SPELLING
ACTIVITY BOOK

Grade 1

Macmillan McGraw-Hill

New York • Farmington

CONTENTS

LEVEL 1

LEVEL 2

LEVEL 3

LEVEL 4, UNIT 1

LEVEL 4, UNIT 2

/a/ -at

c _____

s _____

m _____

h _____

r _____

Directions (to teacher)
Introduce the new phonogram **at** on the chalkboard or with letter cards. Children may be aware that this pattern is also a word. Have them write **at** on the first line. Then have them find the word **cat** in their story. Have them point to the letters **at**. Now they are ready to add **at** to the line to make **cat**. On the chalkboard, demonstrate how you can take off the **c** and add **m** to spell **mat**. When they understand the process, let them complete the page.

Parent/Child Activity
Have your child select three spelling words to illustrate. Have them write each word below its picture.

Macmillan/McGraw-Hill

/a/ -at

Write each spelling word on the line where it belongs.

| cat | mat | sat | hat | rat |

_____

1. c + at _____

_____

2. m + at _____

_____

3. s + at _____

_____

4. h + at _____

_____

5. r + at _____

/al/ -at

Name each picture. Write the letter that makes the beginning sound. Add the **at** of the spelling pattern to complete the word.

1. _____

2. _____

3. _____

4. _____

5. _____

Write a sentence that uses one spelling word.

_____

_____

6

Level 1
Challenge Extension: Have children write or dictate a sentence that uses the words *me* and *you.* Then have them exchange papers with a partner and circle the words *me* and *you* in each other's sentences.

3

/a/ -at

Read the words in the box. Find the words in the puzzle. Draw a circle around each word.

| cat | mat | sat | hat | rat |

t	c	a	t	m	o	i	c	b
m	a	t	t	a	h	i	r	s
t	a	c	m	s	a	t	h	a
h	c	m	s	h	a	t	r	x
a	i	o	t	f	r	a	t	e
n	e	t	f	o	t	m	o	r

5

/a/ -at

Complete each sentence with a spelling word.

1. The cat chased the _____ .

2. I saw an old man in a tall _____ .

3. Bo can tumble on the long _____ .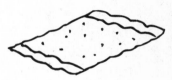

4. The dog _____ at the gate.

5. She sat with two dogs and a striped _____ .

/e/ -ed

_____

- - - - - - - -

_____

_____   _____

- - - - - - - -   - - - - - - - -

r _____   b _____

_____   _____

- - - - - - - -   - - - - - - - -

f _____   l _____

_____

- - - - - - - -

w _____

Directions (to teacher)

Introduce the new phonogram **ed** on the chalkboard or with letter cards. Have children write the letters **ed** on the first line. Then write the word **red** on the chalkboard. Have students write the word **red** on the line. Have children find the color or the word **red** on display around the room. Review the process of adding a consonant to **ed** to make a new word.

Ask for a volunteer to complete the spelling of **bed**, **fed**, and so on. When the process is understood, let children complete the page.

Parent/Child Activity

Ask your child to make up a sentence that uses each spelling word. Help your child as necessary. Then repeat the sentence together.

/e/-ed

Write the **ed** in each problem. Then write the spelling word.

red	bed	fed	led	wed

1. r + _____ = _____

2. b + _____ = _____

3. f + _____ = _____

4. l + _____ = _____

5. w + _____ = _____

/e/-ed

Choose a spelling word to go with each picture.
Write the words on the lines.

red	bed	fed	led	wed

_____

I. _____

_____

2. _____

_____

3. _____

_____

4. _____

_____

5. _____

Challenge Extension: Have children draw a picture of a scene that uses the colors *black* and *blue*. Ask children to write the color words on their drawings.

Level 1

5

/e/-ed

Read the words in the box. Find the words in the puzzle. Draw a circle around each word.

red	**bed**	**fed**	**led**	**wed**

d	e	b	e	f	f	e	d	c
r	e	d	d	e	l	w	e	a
o	h	u	l	e	d	b	e	t
l	l	e	e	w	e	d	e	m
b	b	e	d	d	w	o	d	e
c	a	m	t	w	e	t	r	t

/e/-ed

Write the spelling word that belongs to each sentence.

red	bed	fed	led	wed

_____
- - - - - - -

1. Liza wore a _____ sweater.

_____
- - - - - - -

2. Her big sister _____ the school band.

_____
- - - - - - -

3. Her brother _____ the cat before they left.

_____
- - - - - - -

4. Her mother put a pretty quilt on her _____ .

5. Mrs. Li got the quilt on the day she

_____
- - - - - - -

_____ Mr. Li.

/u/-ut

b _____   n _____

c _____   r _____

h _____

Directions (to teacher)
Introduce the new phonogram **ut** by writing it on the chalkboard. Have children write the letters **ut** on the line. Then have children add the initial consonants to make the spelling words and write them on the lines. Once children are sure of the process, have them complete the page.

Parent/Child Activity
Play a game with your child to practice the use of **but**. Make up phrases such as "Today is sunny." The other must add a contrasting phrase starting with **but**, such as, "but it is growing cloudy." Then have children make up sentences using **cut** and **nut**.

/u/-ut

Add the missing letters to complete each spelling word.
The words are in ABC order.

but	nut	cut	rut	hut

1. b _____

2. c _____

3. h _____

4. n _____

5. r _____

/u/-ut

Find pictures for three of the spelling words. Write the words on the lines.

1. _____   2. _____   3. _____

Use the other two spelling words to complete the sentence.

_____

The car was riding on the old road, _____

_____

then it hit a _____ .

Write a sentence using one of the spelling words.

_____

_____

_____

_____

6

Level 1
Challenge Extension: Have children write or dictate a sentence telling about something they *said* earlier in the day. Then have them write a sentence about two friends, using *and*.

13

/u/-ut

Circle the spelling words in the word puzzle. Then write them on the lines.

but	nut	cut	rut	hut

b u t t e r
t u h u t c
c c u n u t
a u r u t r
c c u t t c

1. _____

2. _____

3. _____

4. _____

5. _____

Level 1   10

Macmillan/McGraw-Hill

/u/-ut

Write the spelling word that belongs in each sentence.

_____
- - - - - - -

1. I found a _____ and I planted it.

_____
- - - - - - -

2. Be careful not to _____ your finger.

_____
- - - - - - -

3. The farm road had a deep _____ in it.

4. The little elf lived in a small brown
_____
- - - - - -
_____ .

_____
- - - - - - -

5. I was ready, _____ I forgot my book.

/o/-ot

```
                        _____
                        - - - - - - - -
                        _____

    _____                        _____
    - - - - - - - -                        - - - - - - - -
n _____                      h _____
    _____                        _____
    - - - - - - - -                        - - - - - - - -
p _____                      c _____
                        _____
                        - - - - - - - -
                    d _____
```

Directions (to teacher)

Introduce the phonogram **ot** on the chalkboard or with letter cards. Have children open to the story "The Chick and the Duckling" and ask them to find the word **not**. Then have them point to the letters **ot**. On the chalkboard, or with movable letters, demonstrate how to take off the first letter of a word in this pattern and use another letter to spell a new word— as **not - n + h = hot**. When they understand the process, let children complete the page.

Parent/Child Activity

Play a game with your child, making up statements about things one should not do: "You should *not* put a *hot pot* on a *cot*." See how many you and your child can make up, using as many spelling words as possible.

Macmillan/McGraw-Hill

/o/-ot

Write a spelling word on each ball.

not	hot	pot	cot	dot

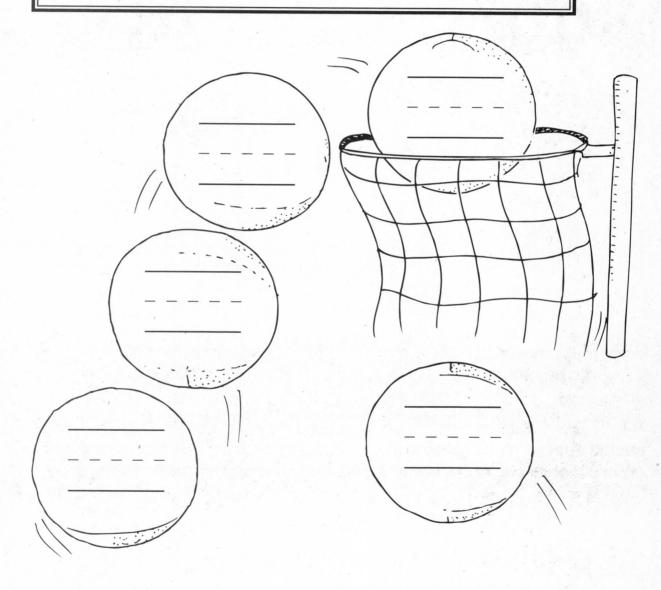

/o/-ot

Name each picture. Write the letter that makes the sound that begins each name. Then, write the **ot** of the spelling pattern to complete the word.

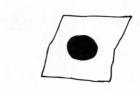

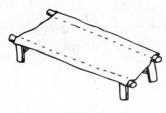

1. _____   2. _____   3. _____

4. _____   5. The fire is _____ .

Write a sentence about a safety rule that uses the word **not**.

_____

_____

_____

_____

Level 1

6

Challenge Extension: Have children draw a picture of something that is *too* big *for* them, *too* small *for* them, *too* high, *too* low, etc. Children may write labels on their pictures, such as "Too Big for Me!"

/o/ -ot

Find the spelling words in the puzzle. Circle the words.

not	hot	pot	cot	dot

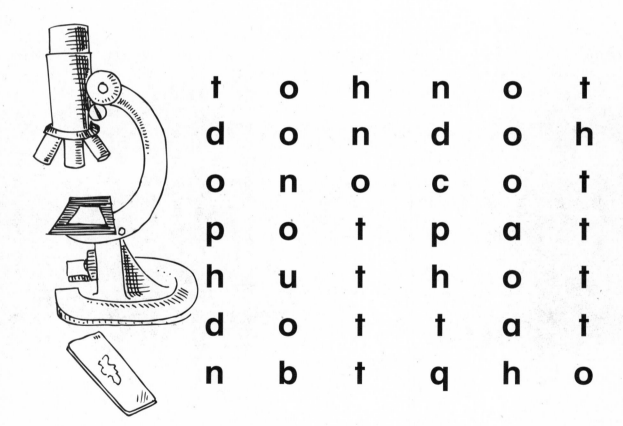

t	o	h	n	o	t
d	o	n	d	o	h
o	n	o	c	o	t
p	o	t	p	a	t
h	u	t	h	o	t
d	o	t	t	a	t
n	b	t	q	h	o

/o/-ot

Use a spelling word to complete each sentence.

1. The coffee _____ was on the stove.

2. The summer day was _____ .

3. Dad put a _____ on the map.

4. We were _____ there yet.

5. At camp I slept on a _____ .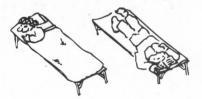

/i/ -id

d _____

l _____

_____

_____

r _____

h _____

k _____

Directions (to teacher)
Introduce the new phonogram **id** on the chalkboard or with letter cards. Ask children to find the word **did** in "The Good Bad Cat." Point to the letters **id**. On the chalkboard, or with movable letters, ask for a volunteer to demonstrate taking off the first letter of a word in this pattern and selecting another letter to spell another word—as **did - d + h = hid**. Then, let children complete the page.

Parent/Child Activity
Try making up question and answer rhymes with your child. One of you might ask "Do you know what I did?" And the other could answer, "I bumped into a kid." Try to make up three questions and answers.

/i/ -id

Complete the spelling word on each egg.

did	hid	lid	kid	rid

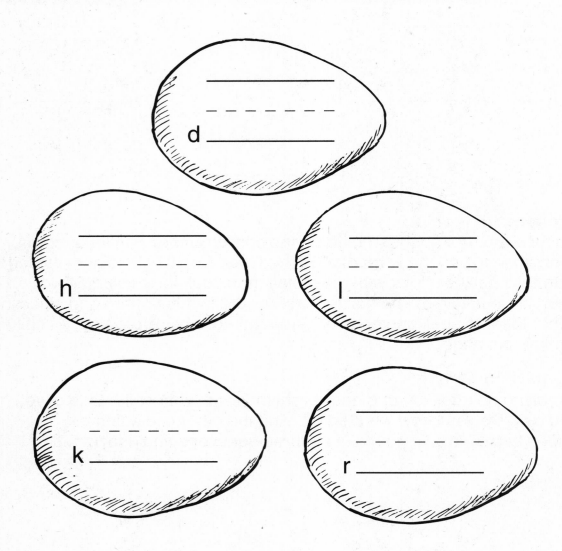

Macmillan/McGraw-Hill

/i/-id

Complete each sentence with a spelling word.

_____

- - - - - - - -

1. A baby goat is called a _____ .

_____

- - - - - - -

2. The red hen _____ her eggs.

_____

- - - - - - -

3. I asked him what he _____ with his hat.

_____

- - - - - - -

4. We need to _____ our streets of trash.

_____

- - - - - - -

5. I cannot find the _____ to this pan.

Level 1

Challenge Extension: To give children practice with the word *on*, have them put an object on another object and say a sentence about it. To practice the word *so*, give children a sentence starter, such as "I got sick...," and have them complete it, using the word *so*.

5

/i/-id

Find the spelling words in the puzzle. Circle them before the monster gets them.

did	hid	lid	kid	rid

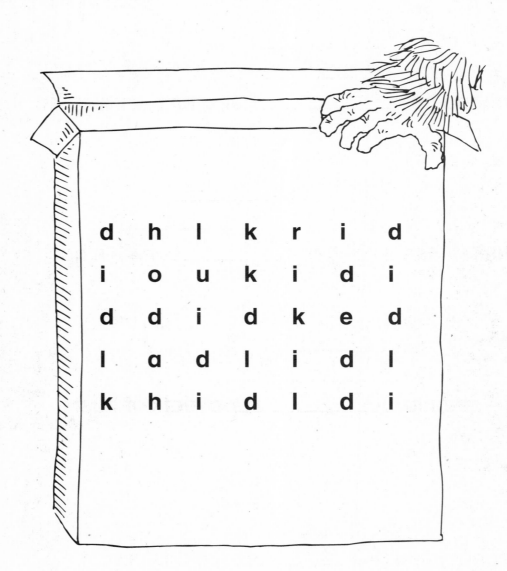

```
d   h   l   k   r   i   d
i   o   u   k   i   d   i
d   d   i   d   k   e   d
l   a   d   l   i   d   l
k   h   i   d   l   d   i
```

/i/ -id

Complete each sentence with a spelling word.

_____

- - - - - - -

1. The kid _____ not want to go in the pen.

_____

2. We bought a new _____ for our pan.

_____

- - - - - - -

3. I found where the hen _____ her eggs.

_____

- - - - - - -

4. The cleaner got _____ of the dirt.

_____

- - - - - - -

5. Our sheep dog pushed the _____ into the pen.

/a/ -ap

```
                    _____
                    - - - - - - -
                    _____

  _____                              _____
  - - - - - - -                            - - - - - - -
n _____                          l  _____
  _____                             _____

  - - - - - - -                           - - - - - - -
t _____                          m  _____

                    _____
                    - - - - - - -
                  c _____
```

Directions (to teacher)

Introduce the new phonogram **ap** on the chalkboard or with letter cards. Ask children to find the word **nap** in the story, "My Friends." Then have them point to the letters **ap**. As before, demonstrate how you can take off the first letter of a word in this pattern and use another letter to spell another word—as **nap - n + l = lap**. If extra practice is still needed, call for volunteers to do the entire sequence on the chalkboard. Then, let children complete the page.

Parent/Child Activity

Help your child make up questions about the spelling words. For example: What is a short sleep called? (nap) What is a drawing of the earth called? (map) What is a type of hat called? (cap)

/a/ -ap

Help the farmer fill the apple basket. Complete each new word on the lines. When you finish each word, you can color the apple with that word.

nap lap tap map cap

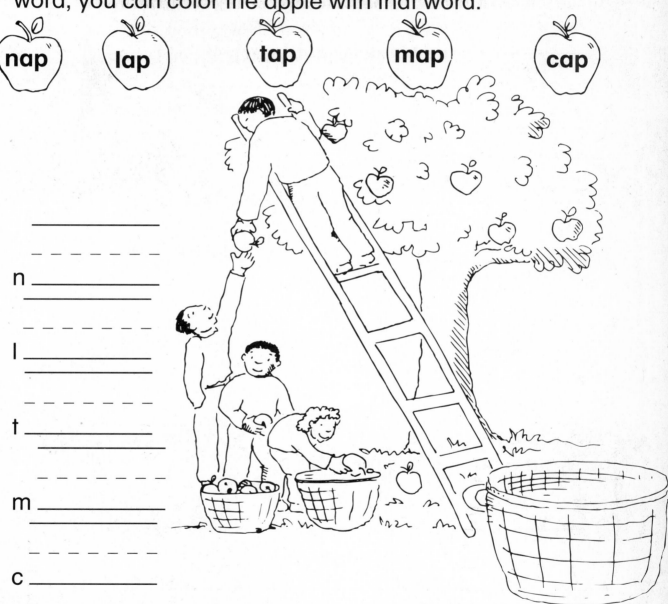

n _____

l _____

t _____

m _____

c _____

/a/-ap

All of the spelling words are in the picture. Write the spelling word on the lines next to the number that matches the number in the picture.

1. _____

2. _____

3. _____

4. _____

5. _____

Now write a sentence about the picture. Use a spelling word.

6. _____

Challenge Extension: Have children draw a picture of themselves running from one place to another. Then have them label their pictures: "I can *run from* _____ to _____.

Level 1

6

/a/ -ap

Find the spelling words in the puzzle. Circle them.
Get the treasure before the pirate does.

p a c c a p o p
l a p l i p i d
z a p t i n a p
g a p m a p e s
p i t o p t a p

/a/-ap

Complete the sentences by writing the spelling words on the lines.

1. The old gray cat liked to _____

   in Grandpa's _____.

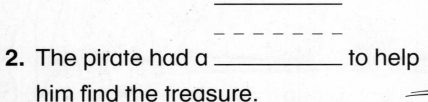

2. The pirate had a _____ to help him find the treasure.

3. To wake him, _____ lightly on his cheek.

4. Mia lost her baseball _____.

5

/e/ -et

_____

_ _ _ _ _ _ _ _ _ _

_____

_____   _____

_ _ _ _ _ _ _ _ _   _ _ _ _ _ _ _ _ _

g _____   b _____

_____

_ _ _ _ _ _ _ _ _   _ _ _ _ _ _ _ _ _

m _____   l _____

_____

_ _ _ _ _ _ _ _ _

p _____

Directions (to teacher)

Introduce the new phonogram **et** on the chalkboard or with letter cards. Have children open their readers and point to some of the places where they find the word **bet** in "Bet You Can't." Call on individuals to demonstrate how to take off the first letter of a word in this pattern and use another letter to spell another word—as **bet - b + g = get**. Ask if anyone can name more words in this pattern. You may wish to include **jet**, **net**, **wet**, and **set**. Then, let children complete the page.

Parent/Child Activity

Help your child make up a silly rhyme that uses at least two of the spelling words. For example: I hope my mother will _let_ me _get_ the _pet_ that I _met_ in the _pet_ shop.

Macmillan/McGraw-Hill

/e/-et

Lee needs ladybugs for her flowers. Fill in the missing letters to make each spelling word.

get **bet** **met** **let** **pet**

_____

m _____

l _____

p _____

g _____

b _____

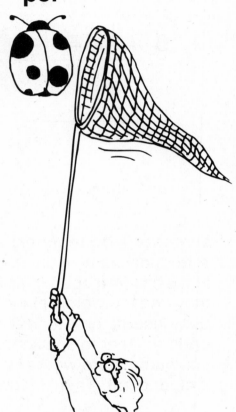

Level 2   5

/e/-et

Complete each sentence with a spelling word.

_____
_ _ _ _ _ _ _

1. Win and Pete _____ after school to play ball.

_____
_ _ _ _ _ _ _

2. The teacher _____ me pass out the papers.

_____
_ _ _ _ _ _ _

3. Jameka's _____ is a tiny brown mouse.

_____
_ _ _ _ _ _ _

4. Corky went to the store to _____ more bananas.

_____
_ _ _ _ _ _ _

5. I _____ you can't finish before I do.

Level 2

Challenge Extension: To practice the word *are*, have children draw and label a picture of something they and a friend are doing: "We *are* playing ball." To practice the word *can*, have children draw and label a picture of something they can do: "I *can* tie my shoelaces."

5

33

Name: _____ Date: _____

/e/-et

Find the spelling words in the puzzle ring. Circle
each spelling word. Then write the words.

get	bet	met	let	pet

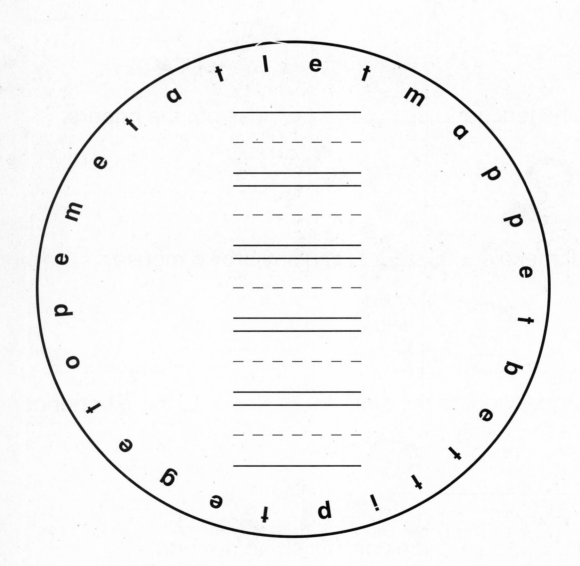

/e/ -et

Fill in the crossword puzzles with the spelling words. You have one surprise word.

Across

1. I _____ I can swim.

Down

2. I _____ my friend after school.

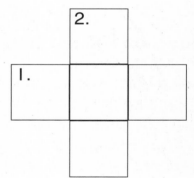

Across

1. My dog is my _____.

Down

2. I _____ the vet pet my dog.

Across

1. I will _____ the ball.

Down

2. I hit the ball over the _____.

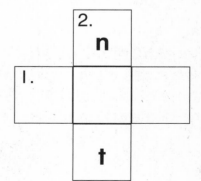

Macmillan/McGraw-Hill

/i/ -ill

_____

- - - - - - - - - - - -

_____

_____   _____

- - - - - - - - -   - - - - - - - - -

h _____   f _____
                                     _____

- - - - - - - - -   - - - - - - - - -

gr _____   b _____

_____

- - - - - - - - - - - -

w _____

Directions (to teacher)

Introduce the new phonogram **ill** on the chalkboard or with letter cards.
Ask a volunteer to point out how this pattern differs from the earlier ones. It
should be noted that the final consonant sound is spelled with a double
letter: **ll**. Also, children may realize that the pattern itself, **ill**, makes a word.
Call on individuals to demonstrate how you can take off the first letter of a
word in this pattern and use another letter to spell another word—as **hill - h
+ f = fill**. Ask if anyone knows of any more words in this pattern. Common
ones are **spill**, **mill**, **skill**, **pill**, and **thrill**. Less common words are **dill**,
chill, **gill**, and **quill**. Then, let children complete the page.

Parent/Child Activity

Use these familiar new words to make up silly rhymes with your child: I cut
some wood to *fill* the *grill*. I carried the wood up a *hill*. (One trick to making
rhymes work is to use the same number of syllables in each line.)

/i/ –ill

Climb the steps to the treehouse. Choose the word that is spelled correctly in each pair. Write the word on the line.

grill
gril

holl
hill

wiil
will

fil
fill

bill
bil

/i/ -ill

Write the spelling word that tells about each picture.

1. _____

2. _____

3. _____

4. _____

5. Howie said, "I _____ do it!"

Macmillan/McGraw-Hill

Challenge Extension: Have children write or dictate a funny sentence, using the words *one* and *very*: "I have *one very* small dog." Children may illustrate their sentences, as well.

Level 2

5

/i/ -ill

Find the spelling words in the story below. Circle them. Then write them on the lines. Some words are used more than once. You should have seven circles in all.

hill	fill	grill	bill	will

I bet I can climb that hill. I will wear my cap with a bill to shade my nose. At the top, I will take it off and fill it with good rocks. If I bring you some, will you grill a hot dog for me?

1. _____

2. _____

3. _____

4. _____

5. _____

6. _____

7. _____

/i/ -ill

Complete the story. Write the spelling words on the lines.

_____
- - - - - - - - - - -

One day, Dad said, "I _____ take you

all out to eat. We will go to the new place at the top
_____
- - - - - - - - - -

of the _____ . They have a big open
_____
- - - - - - - - - - - - -

_____ for cooking. I hope you will
_____
- - - - - - - - -

_____ up on good food."
_____
- - - - - - - - -

After the meal, the waiter gave Dad the _____ .

/i/ -ig

_____

- - - - - - -

_____

_____

- - - - - -

p _____
_____
_____

- - - - - -

d _____

_____

- - - - - -

w _____
_____
_____

- - - - - -

b _____

_____

- - - - -

f _____

Directions (to teacher)
Introduce the new phonogram **ig** on the chalkboard or with letter cards. Call on individuals to find **ig** words in "Down by the Bay" and to demonstrate how you can take off the first letter of a word in this pattern and use another letter to spell another word—as **pig - p + w = wig**. Ask if anyone can name other words that follow this pattern. Less common words, but known to some, might be **gig**, **rig**, **jig**, **twig**, and **sprig**. Then, let children complete the page.

Parent/Child Activity
Ask your child to draw pictures for the new spelling words. With the words beneath each picture, the drawings could be part of your child's personal dictionary.

/i/ -ig

Write the spelling word that begins with the same
sound you hear at the beginning of each picture name.

1. _____

2. _____

3. _____

4. _____

5. _____

/i/ -ig

Write the spelling word that belongs in each sentence.

big	wig	fig	pig	dig

1. The opposite of small is _____.

2. We _____ a hole in the sand.

3. A _____ is a farm animal.

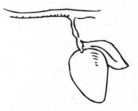

4. A _____ is a fruit from a tree.

5. A _____ is hair that you wear.

Macmillan/McGraw-Hill

Level 2
Challenge Extension: Have children write or dictate a question beginning with the phrase:
"*Do* you want to *go* ...?" Children may complete the question in their own way.

5

43

/i/ -ig

Jake is fishing. Help him catch five fish.

Find the spelling words in the puzzle. Circle them.
The words may go down or across.

| pig | wig | dig | big | fig |

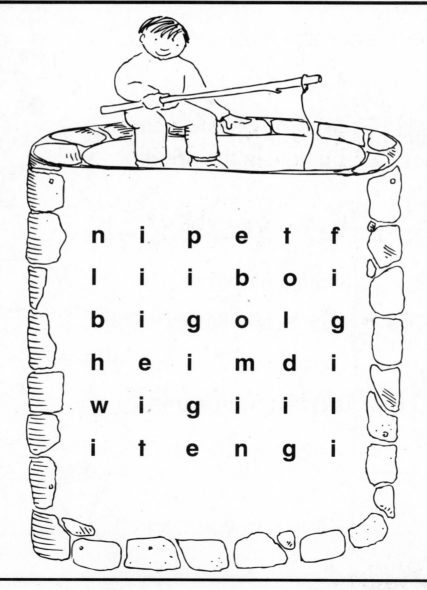

n	i	p	e	t	f
l	i	i	b	o	i
b	i	g	o	l	g
h	e	i	m	d	i
w	i	g	i	i	l
i	t	e	n	g	i

/i/ -ig

Use the spelling words to complete the sentences.
Write the word you need on each line.

pig	wig	dig	big	fig

_____

- - - - - - -

1. Bess wanted to _____ a hole.

_____

- - - - - - -

2. Barney ate a _____ as he watched.

_____

- - - - - - -

3. The hole was _____ and deep.

_____

- - - - - - -

4. It was big enough to hold a big _____ .

_____

- - - - - - -

5. Bess found a _____ to put on the pig.

/u/-ug

_____

- - - - - - -

_____   _____

- - - - - - -   - - - - - - -

d _____   sl _____

_____   _____

- - - - - - -   - - - - - - -

pl _____   b _____

_____

- - - - - - -

h _____

Directions (to teacher)

Introduce the new phonogram **ug** on the chalkboard or with letter cards. Call on individuals to find some of the words in the story, "Jasper's Beanstalk." Ask a volunteer to demonstrate how you can take off the first letter of a word in this pattern and use another letter to spell another word—as **dug - d + sl = slug**. Elicit more familiar words that follow this pattern: **tug**, **jug**, **mug**, **rug**, **snug**, **shrug**. Then, let children complete the page.

Parent/Child Activity

Tell your child about the saying, "snug as a bug in a rug."
Help your child make up other rhyming sentences with the spelling words.

Macmillan/McGraw-Hill

/u/-ug

dug	slug	plug	bug	hug

Write the spelling words that begin with **b**, **d**, and **h**.

1. _____

2. _____

3. _____

Write the spelling words that begin with **pl** and **sl**.

4. _____

5. _____

Read the spelling problems. Then write the answers.

6. h + ug = _____   7. sl + ug = _____

8. m + ug = _____

/u/-ug

Write the spelling word that belongs in each sentence.

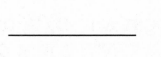

_____

1. Our dog _____ that hole in my garden.

_____

2. A _____ left that slimy trail.

_____

3. One big green _____ flew in the door.

_____

4. Aunt Tilly gives me a _____ when she visits.

_____

5. Tom found a rock to _____ the hole in the wall.

Macmillan/McGraw-Hill

Challenge Extension: Have children write or dictate a sentence about a person they know, using the phrase: "*He* is happy *when* he ..."

Level 2

5

/u/ -ug

Help the beanstalk grow leaves. Draw a leaf circle around each spelling word you find.

g u b u g z d i

l s l u g a t s

u h u g j k l u

m d u g g u u h

p l u g x w h t

/u/ -ug

Use the spelling words to complete the silly rhyme.
Write the words on the lines.

dug	Slug	plug	Bug	hug

_____

Little Sylvester the _____

_____

Said to his friend Billy _____ ,

_____

"This home that I _____ is quite snug.

_____

I _____ in my lamp

To keep out the damp.

_____

Now my home is as warm as a _____ ."

/i/ -ick

_____

- - - - - - - - - - - - - - -

_____

_____   _____

- - - - - - - - - - - - - - -   - - - - - - - - - - - - - - -

ch_____   tr_____

_____   _____

- - - - - - - - - - - - - - -   - - - - - - - - - - - - - - -

st_____   k_____

_____

- - - - - - - - - - - - - - -

br_____

Directions (to teacher)

Introduce the new phonogram **ick** on the chalkboard or with letter cards. Tie the spelling activity to the language pattern of the story, "An Egg Is an Egg." For example: A word is a word until you change a letter. Then it becomes a new word. Ask a volunteer to demonstrate how to take off the first two letters of a word ending with a phonogram and use another letter or pair of letters to spell a new word—as **chick - ch + st = stick**. Elicit additional words in this pattern: **lick, sick, tick, wick, click, slick, prick, thick**. Then, let children complete the page.

Parent/Child Activity

Talk about the words *chick*, *stick*, and *brick* with your child. Ask: Which things feel hard? Which thing feels soft? Talk about the words *trick* and *kick* by asking: Name a game where you *kick* a ball. What kind of *trick* can you teach a dog?

Macmillan/McGraw-Hill

/i/-ick

One word in each pair is wrong. Choose the right word to complete each sentence.

_____
\- \- \- \- \- \- \- \-

1. By the henhouse was a yellow _____.
     cick   chick

_____
\- \- \- \- \- \- \- \-

2. A _____ is red and thick.

     brick   brik

_____
\- \- \- \- \- \- \- \-

3. The _____ to the game is to be quick.

     tick   trick

_____
\- \- \- \- \- \- \- \-

4. Send the ball far with a hard _____.

     kick   kik

_____
\- \- \- \- \- \- \- \-

5. Use a _____ to stir the paint.

     stick   sick

/i/ -ick

Look at each picture. Use a spelling word to complete the sentence next to each one.

chick	stick	brick	trick	Kick

1. What a good _____ !

2. _____ the ball!

3. Go under the _____ .

4. See that little yellow _____ .

5. We live in a red _____ house.

Macmillan/McGraw-Hill

5

Level 3
Challenge Extension: To provide practice with *we* and *some*, have children say several complete sentences, telling about something they do in class: *We* read *some* books. *We* play *some* games.

53

/i/ -ick

Use the spelling words to complete the puzzle.

| trick | chick | kick | brick | stick |

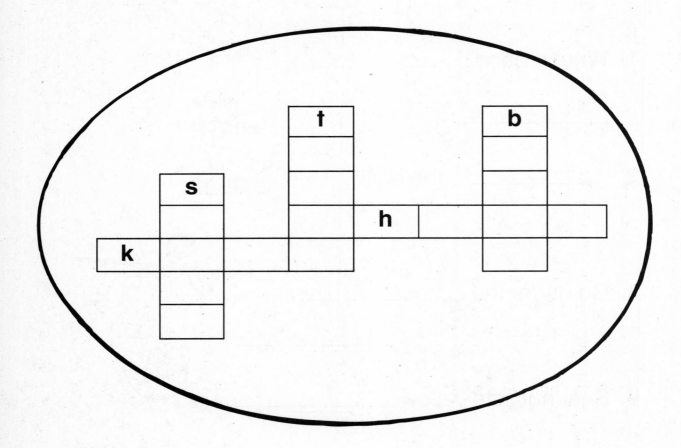

/i/-ick

Read each sentence.
Write the correct word on each line.

chick	stick	brick	trick	kick

1. A _____ grows inside an egg.

2. I used a _____ to make a wall.

3. Dan showed me how to do that magic
_____.

4. Take a step before you _____.

5. Find a thick _____ to use for a
pole.

You can add **s** to all of the spelling words to make
other words. Write a sentence about bricks or tricks
or chicks on another piece of paper.

/i/ -it

_____

- - - - - - - -

_____

b_____   p_____

- - - - - - -   - - - - - - -

h_____   s_____

Directions (to teacher)
Introduce the new phonogram **it** on the chalkboard or with letter cards. This is another pattern that is also a word independent of other letters. Ask a volunteer to demonstrate how to add letters to this pattern to spell other words—as **s + it = sit**, and then **sit - s + p = pit**. Elicit other words with this pattern: **fit, kit, lit, wit**. Some may also know: **knit** or **slit**. Then, let children complete the page.

Parent/Child Activity
Help your child make up silly sentences, using as many of the spelling words as possible.

Macmillan/McGraw-Hill

/i/ -it

Write the spelling words that begin with **b, h, p,** and **s.**

1. _____   2. _____

3. _____   4. _____

Read the spelling problems. Then write the answers.

5. pit - p + f = _____

6. bit - b + h = _____

7. sit - s + k = _____

8. Write the little word that is in all of the spelling

words. _____

/i/ -it

Write the spelling word to complete each sentence.

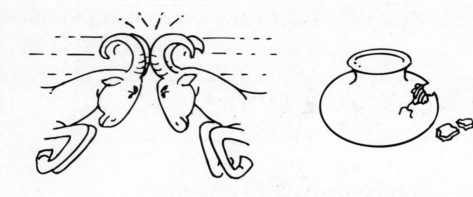

_____
— — — — — — —

1. The opposite of stand is _____.

_____
— — — — — — —

2. When two things bump, they _____.

_____
— — — — — — —

3. A big hole is called a _____.

_____
— — — — — — —

4. A piece of something is a _____ of it.

_____
— — — — — — —

5. I want to know, where is _____?

Challenge Extension: Have children draw or cut out a picture of an object, a person, or an animal and complete the following sentence about it: *"This is a _____."*

58

5

Macmillan/McGraw-Hill

/il/-it

Read across or down to find the hidden spelling words.

Circle each spelling word you find.

l	e	t	s	e	t	a	p	s
n	h	s	i	t	l	i	l	t
t	i	p	r	k	o	i	t	p
g	t	i	b	i	t	j	m	u
r	x	t	i	l	u	q	u	i
q	p	z	t	e	w	u	x	v

Write one of your spelling words in a sentence.

_____

- -

_____

_____

- -

_____

/i/ -it

Name each picture. Write a spelling word that begins with the same sound you hear at the beginning of each picture name.

1. _____

2. _____

3. _____

4. _____

Write the spelling word that is in each word you wrote above.

5. _____

/ā/ -ade

_____

- - - - - - - - - - - - - -

_____

_____

- - - - - - - - - - - - - -

bl _____   **tr** _____

_____

- - - - - - - - - - - - - -

gr _____   **m** _____

_____

- - - - - - - - - - - - - -

w _____

Directions (to teacher)

Introduce the new phonogram **ade** on the chalkboard or with letter cards. Call on children to find words with this pattern in their readers. Ask a volunteer to demonstrate how to take off the first letters of a word in this pattern and use other letters to spell another word—as **blade - bl + gr = grade**. Elicit additional words in this pattern: **shade, fade, jade**. If working with rhymes produces words such as *maid, paid, laid, played*, point out that those are spelled with different patterns which they will learn later. Then, let children complete the page.

Parent/Child Activity

Help your child make up a story using at least three of their spelling words. You may want to use this story starter: "Once upon a time there was a girl in the first *grade* who *made* the most beautiful pictures...."

/ā/-ade

The starting letters are **w**, **gr**, **bl**, **m**, and **tr**. Write the spelling words in ABC order.

1. _____

2. _____

3. _____

4. _____

5. _____

Write the three spelling words that are spelled with five letters.

6. _____ 7. _____

8. _____

/āl/-ade

Read the sentences. Use a spelling word to complete each sentence.

_____
- - - - - - - - - - - - - - -
I. I like to _____ baseball cards.

_____
- - - - - - - - - - - - - - -
2. Ben _____ a good trade for a
new football card.

_____
- - - - - - - - - - - - - - -
3. The bread knife has a very sharp_____.

_____
- - - - - - - - - - - - - - -
4. What _____ are you in this year?

_____
- - - - - - - - - - - - - - -
5. My puppy loves to _____ in puddles.

Level 3
Challenge Extension: Have children write or dictate two sentences about a pet they have or a pet they
would like to have, using the words *goes* and *knows*: "My puppy *goes* to the park with me. My puppy
knows his name."

5

63

Macmillan/McGraw-Hill

/ā/ -ade

Find the five spelling words on the shell. Circle
each word you find.

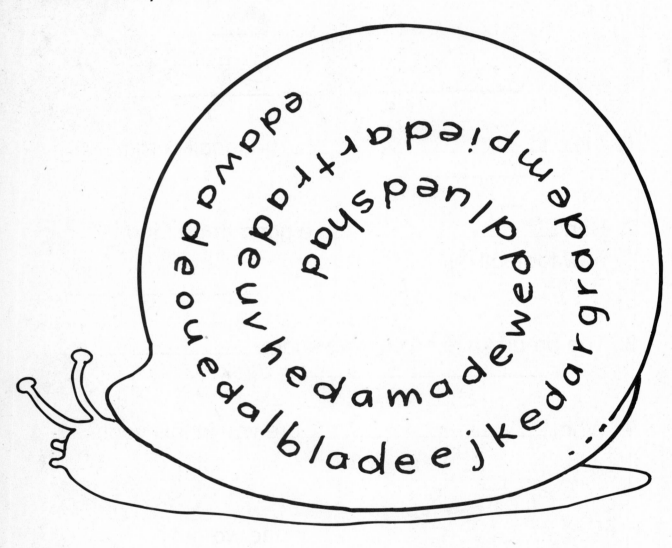

/ā/-ade

Read the sentences. Use a spelling word to complete each sentence.

_____
- - - - - - - - - - - - - -

1. Have you ever seen a _____

of grass?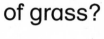

_____
- - - - - - - - - - - - - -

2. I am in first _____.

_____
- - - - - - - - - - - - - -

3. I will _____ my book

for your book.

_____
- - - - - - - - - - - - - -

4. I can _____ in the water.

_____
- - - - - - - - - - - - - -

5. I _____ a necklace.

Macmillan/McGraw-Hill

/ā/-ake

```
        _____
        - - - - - - - - -
        _____

  _____              _____
  - - - - - - - -              - - - - - - - -
m_____            l_____

  _____              _____
  - - - - - - - -              - - - - - - - -
t_____            b_____

        _____
        - - - - - - - - -
      c_____
```

Directions (to teacher)

Introduce the new phonogram **ake** on the chalkboard or with letter cards. Call on children to find words with this pattern in their readers. Ask a volunteer to demonstrate how to take off the first letter of a word in this pattern and use another letter to spell a new word—as **make - m + t = take**. Elicit additional words in this pattern: **fake**, **wake**, **snake**. Then, let children complete the page.

Parent/Child Activity

Help your child make up a sentence for each spelling word. Ask your child to repeat each sentence aloud.

Macmillan/McGraw-Hill

/ā/-ake

Help the little pig build his house. Write the letters of the spelling pattern in the top box.

Fill in the letters to spell the new words.

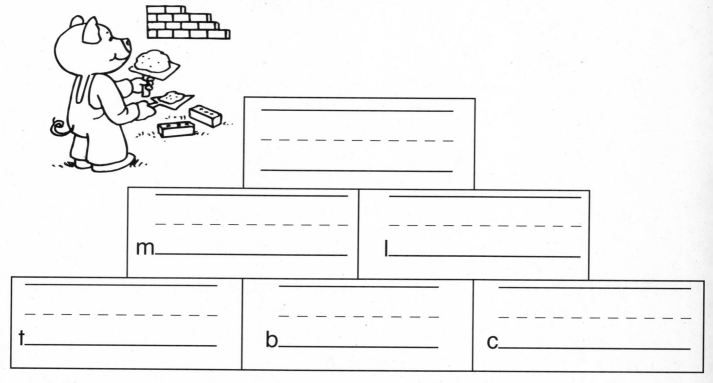

m_____   l_____

t_____   b_____   c_____

Solve these word puzzles.

make - m + sn = _____

snake - sn + br = _____

/ā/-ake

Read the story. Use the spelling words to complete the story.

Dee woke up early and called her cousin Bee.
_____

— — — — — — — — — —
"If you will _____ two sandwiches, _____
_____

— — — — — — — —   — — — — — — — — —
I will _____ a carrot _____.
_____

— — — — — — — — —
Then we can _____ a picnic basket
_____ "

— — — — — — — — —
down by the _____.

Challenge Extension: To provide practice with the words *how* and *about*, have children complete the following sentences: "I know *how* to_____. I want to learn *about*_____."

Level 3

5

/ā/ -ake

Read the sentences. Use a spelling word to complete each sentence. Use the answers to complete the puzzle.

Across

3. The opposite of give is ____.

5. Water bigger than a pond may be a ____.

Down

1. There are candles on a birthday ____.

2. The opposite of break is ____.

4. To make bread, you must ____.

/ā/-ake

Did you ever help to bake a cake? What things did you need? Where did you take your cake to eat it? Write a story about a special cake. Use four of your spelling words.

_____

- -

_____

- -

_____

- -

_____

- -

_____

/ī/ -ime

Pretest Directions
Fold back the paper in half. Use the blanks to write each word as it is read aloud. When you finish the test, unfold the paper. Use the list at the right to correct any spelling mistakes. Practice the words you missed for the Final Test.

To Parents
Here are the results of your child's weekly spelling Pretest. You can help your child study for the Final Test by following these simple steps for each word on the list:

I. Read the word to your child.

2. Have your child write the word, saying each letter as it is written.

3. Say each letter of the word as your child checks the spelling.

4. If a mistake has been made, have your child read each letter of the correctly spelled word aloud and then repeat steps 1-3.

Parent/Child Activity
Ask your child to point to the three letters that are the same in each word. Then ask your child to say and write each word.

I. _____

2. _____

3. _____

4. _____

5. _____

I. time

2. dime

3. chime

4. grime

5. lime

Challenge Words

_____

_____

Challenge Words

two

help

/ī/ -ime

Write the letters that are in all of the spelling words.

1. _____ _____ _____

Add the missing letters for each spelling word.

2. t _____ _____ _____

3. _____ _____ i m e

4. _____ _____ i m e

5. d _____ _____ _____

6. l _____ _____ _____

Write the words in the spelling list in ABC order.

7. _____   8. _____

9. _____   10. _____

11. _____

Add an **s** to one of your spelling words to make a new word.

12. _____

/ī/-*ime*

Write the correct spelling word to complete each sentence.

1. Amy could tell _____.

2. Tim lost a _____.

3. Tasha ate a green _____.

4. Bob hears the bell _____.

5. Ella washed off _____.

Write the word for each riddle.

6. It begins like and it rhymes

   with **grime**. _____

7. It begins like and it rhymes

   with **dime**. _____

8. It begins like and it rhymes

   with **lime**. _____

Macmillan/McGraw-Hill

8

Level 4/Unit 1
Challenge Extension: To provide practice with the words *two* and *help*, have children complete the following sentence: "*Two* ways that I *help* at home are to _____ and _____."

/ī/ -ime

Finding Mistakes

Find five mistakes in this poem and circle them.
Write the words correctly on the lines.

In my pocket, i found a nickel and diem.

I used them to buy a lemon and lim.

i took some water and added ice,

And I mad a drink that tasted nice.

1. _____ 2. _____

3. _____ 4. _____

5. _____

Use your rhyming spelling words to complete this
short poem. Then add one more line.

6. The numbers tell the _____.

7. The clock rings out its _____.

8. _____

_____

Macmillan/McGraw-Hill

/ī/-*ime*

Fix these mixed-up letters to make spelling words.

meit   ergim   emid   hecim   ilem

1. _____ 2. _____

3. _____ 4. _____

5. _____

Fill in the squares to complete the spelling words.

/ī/ -ice

Pretest Directions
Fold back the paper in half. Use the blanks to write each word as it is read aloud. When you finish the test, unfold the paper. Use the list at the left to correct any spelling mistakes. Practice the words you missed for the Final Test.

To Parents
Here are the results of your child's weekly spelling Pretest. You can help your child study for the Final Test by following these simple steps for each word on the list:

1. Read the word to your child.

2. Have your child write the word, saying each letter as it is written.

3. Say each letter of the word as your child checks the spelling.

4. If a mistake has been made, have your child read each letter of the correctly spelled word aloud and then repeat steps 1-3.

Parent/Child Activity
Ask your child to write the words in ABC order. (ice, mice, nice, rice, slice)

1. nice

2. mice

3. rice

4. slice

5. ice

1. _____

2. _____

3. _____

4. _____

5. _____

Challenge Words

much

was

Challenge Words

_____

_____

/ī/-ice

Write on the lines a spelling word that belongs in each group.

Food	Animals	Something Cold
1. _____	2. _____	3. _____

All of these words have an **i** and an **e** in them.

4. Which letter says its name?   _____

5. Which letter is silent?   _____

Circle the word pairs that are rhymes. Write the words that rhyme.

ice	nine	dice	slice	rise
I'm	hot	mice	nice	rice

6. _____   _____

7. _____   _____

8. Which letters are in all of the spelling words?

_____   _____   _____

/ī/ -ice

Write the spelling word to answer each question.

1. Which word means more than one mouse? _____

2. Which word means a kind of food? _____

3. Which word means frozen water? _____

4. Which word means something good? _____

5. Which word means a thin piece cut off a bigger

one? _____

Write spelling words in the story.

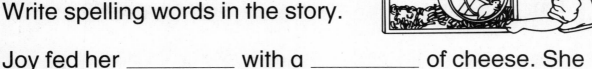

Joy fed her _____ with a _____ of cheese. She

keeps the cheese on _____ so it will be _____ for

her pets to eat. Then she has _____ pudding for her

own lunch.

Word Journal

Write the spelling words in your Word Journal.
Write a meaning for each word.

Challenge Extension: To provide practice with the word *was*, have children complete the following pair of sentences: "Now, I am_____ years old. Last year I *was* _____ years old." To practice the word *much*, have children complete the following sentence: "I like _____ very *much*."

Level 4/Unit 1

10

Macmillan/McGraw-Hill

/ī/-ice

Tammy wrote a silly poem with her spelling words, but she made some mistakes. Circle each mistake. Then write the words correctly on the lines.

The little mise

like to slide on the ise.

For supper They eat

a slise of cheese

with brown riece.

1. _____   2. _____   3. _____

4. _____   5. _____

Writing Activity

If you had pet mice, what would you feed them? Write a story to tell about it. Use as many spelling words as you can.

_____

_____

_____

/ī/-ice

Write the spelling word answer for each word math puzzle.

1. m + ice =

2. mice – m + n =

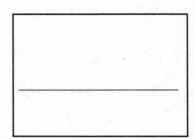

3. nice – n + sl =

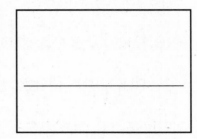

4. slice – sl =

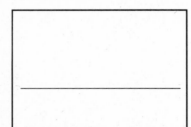

5. r + ice =

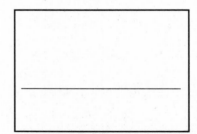

Now, write the letters **tw**, **pr**, and **sp** on the lines below to make three new words.

_____ **ice**   _____ **ice**   _____**ice**

Write a sentence that uses two of the words you made.

_____

_____

Macmillan/McGraw-Hill

/ē/-eep

Pretest Directions
Fold back the paper in half. Use the blanks to write each word as it is read aloud. When you finish the test, unfold the paper. Use the list at the right to correct any spelling mistakes. Practice the words you missed for the Final Test.

To Parents
Here are the results of your child's weekly spelling Pretest. You can help your child study for the Final Test by following these simple steps for each word on the list:

I. Read the word to your child.

2. Have your child write the word, saying each letter as it is written.

3. Say each letter of the word as your child checks the spelling.

4. If a mistake has been made, have your child read each letter of the correctly spelled word aloud and then repeat steps I–3.

Parent/Child Activity
Ask your child to find another familiar word that is spelled with this pattern. (deep, peep, steep, sweep, weep)

I. _____

2. _____

3. _____

4. _____

5. _____

Challenge Words

_____

_____

I. sheep

2. sleep

3. keep

4. creep

5. jeep

Challenge Words

into

them

/ē/-eep

1. Write the three letters that are used in all of the

   spelling words. _____ _____ _____

2. Make a new word by changing the **k** of **keep** to **j**.

   _____

Begin with the letters **j** and then **sh**, **sl**, and **cr**. Add
eep to spell four new words.

3. _____   4. _____

5. _____   6. _____

Circle the pairs that rhyme. Write the pairs.

deep	steep	keep	wipe	sheep
keen	shell	sleep	weep	creep

7. _____

8. _____

/ē/-eep

Complete each sentence with the right spelling word.

1. More than one sheep are called _____.

2. When you hold onto something, you

_____ it.

3. To move very slowly is to _____.

4. When you are tired, go to _____.

5. A small car that can drive on a dirt road is a

_____.

Write the word that goes with each picture.

6. _____

7. _____

8. _____

9. _____

Write the word that is the opposite of give away.

10. _____

Macmillan/McGraw-Hill

10

Level 4/Unit 1
Challenge Extension: Give children oral practice with the words *into* and *them* by having them say and complete the following sentences: "I bit *into* the _____. I came *into* the _____. I gave *them* to _____. I will meet *them* _____."

/ē/-eep

Finding Mistakes

Bob wrote a good story, but he made six mistakes. Circle the mistakes. Write the words correctly on the lines.

The sheeps were coming in from the hills. they moved very slowly. They seemed to crep along. One was almost hit when a jipe sped over the ranch road. Last night, I went to sleepe. I dreamed that the rancher gave mi a baby lamb to keep.

1. _____ 2. _____

3. _____ 4. _____

5. _____ 6. _____

Writing Activity

Write a sentence to tell about the picture.

Use two spelling words.

_____

_____

_____

/ē/-eep

Write the spelling words that begin with **sh** and **sl**.

1. _____   2. _____

Write the spelling words that begin with **cr** and with **k**.

3. _____   4. _____

Write the spelling word that means a kind of car.

5. _____

Find your spelling words in the block of letters. Circle the words. One is on a slant.

```
c  l  s  s  t
p  j  h  l  a
l  k  e  e  p
c  r  e  e  p
k  n  p  p  p
```

/ī/-y

Pretest Directions
Fold back the paper in half. Use the blanks to write each word as it is read aloud. When you finish the test, unfold the paper. Use the list at the left to correct any spelling mistakes. Practice the words you missed for the Final Test.

To Parents
Here are the results of your child's weekly spelling Pretest. You can help your child study for the Final Test by following these simple steps for each word on the word list:

1. Read the word to your child.

2. Have your child write the word, saying each letter as it is written.

3. Say each letter of the word as your child checks the spelling.

4. If a mistake has been made, have your child read each letter of the correctly spelled word aloud and then repeat steps 1–3.

Parent/Child Activity
Ask your child to say another familiar word with the final **y**. (by, cry, dry, why, spy) Encourage them to use each word in a sentence.

1. sky

2. shy

3. fly

4. my

5. try

1. _____

2. _____

3. _____

4. _____

5. _____

Challenge Words

her

she

Challenge Words

_____

_____

/ī/ -y

Read the words. Circle the letter that is the same in each word.

1. fly   **2.** my   **3.** shy

4. sky   **5.** try

Now, on each line, write the letter that completes the spelling word.

6. sh_____   **7.** m_____   **8.** sk _____

9. fl_____   **10.** tr_____

Read the sentences. Circle the words that have the same sound you hear in **my**.

I heard the mouse cry when the owl flew by.

The bird could fly in the dark night sky.

Write the words you circled that spell the sound with a final **y**.

11. _____   **12.** _____

13. _____   **14.** _____

/ī/-y

Some of the spelling words don't make sense in these sentences. Circle the wrong words. Write the correct words on the lines.

1. Peter Pan was able to sky.   _____

2. There were many clouds in the blue shy.   _____

3. I fly to do my best at all times.   _____

4. I need new laces for by sneakers.   _____

Write the spelling word to complete each sentence.

5. The air above us is called the _____.

6. If the toy belongs to me, I call it _____ toy.

7. When I meet someone new, sometimes I feel a

   little _____.

8. Something a bird can do is _____.

Challenge Extension: Have children write two sentences about Chicken Licken, using the words *she* and *her*.

Level 4/Unit 1

12

Macmillan/McGraw-Hill

/ī/-y

Finding Mistakes

Lee did not have time to check her writing. Find her mistakes and circle them. Write the correct words on the lines.

1. Shy Kim walked bi the tall clock. _____

2. She saw a fli creeping up the side of the clock.

   _____

3. kim said, "Hi, Fly! You'd better fly away fast."

   _____

4. Your home is in the ski. _____

5. You should not be in mi house. _____

Writing Activity

Write sentences to tell about a fly you found in your house. Use at least two of the spelling words.

_____

_____

_____

_____

/ī/-y

I. Write the spelling word that begins with **fl**.

_____

2. Write the spelling word that rhymes with **dry** and

begins like  .

_____

3. Write the spelling word that begins like  .

_____

4. Write the spelling word that begins like 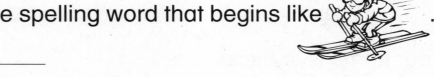 .

_____

5. Write the spelling word that begins like **mine**.

_____

Write the missing letters to complete the spelling words.
When you are done, the words will be in ABC order.

6. f_____   **7.** _____y

8. sh_____   **9.** s_____

10. _____y

/āl-ame

Pretest
Fold back the paper in half. Use the blanks to write each word as it is read aloud. When you finish the test, unfold the paper. Use the list at the right to correct any spelling mistakes. Practice the words you missed for the Final Test.

To Parents
Here are the results of your child's weekly spelling Pretest. You can help your child study for the Final Test by following these simple steps for each word on the list:

1. Read the word to your child.

2. Have your child write the word, saying each letter as it is written.

3. Say each letter of the word as your child checks the spelling.

4. If a mistake has been made, have your child read each letter of the correctly spelled word aloud and then repeat steps 1–3.

Parent/Child Activity
Ask your child to write the three letters that are the same in each word. Work with your child to make as many words with the **ame** pattern as possible.

1. _____
2. _____
3. _____
4. _____
5. _____

1. came
2. same
3. game
4. name
5. frame

Challenge Words

_____

_____

Challenge Words

just

home

/ā/-ame

came	same	game	name	frame

Write the spelling words in ABC order. Then circle
the letters that are the same in each word.

1. _____   **2.** _____

3. _____   **4.** _____

5. _____

6. All of these spelling words have the letters

_____.

Add the letters to complete each word.

7. c _____ m _____   **8.** sam _____

9. gam _____   **10.** n _____ _____ _____

/ā/ -ame

Read each sentence. Write the spelling word to complete each sentence.

1. Things that are alike are the _____ .

2. Soccer is a good _____ .

3. Rocky Smith is his _____ .

4. That picture is in a wooden _____ .

5. She _____ to my party on Saturday.

Write the spelling words. Follow the directions.

6. Change the **fr** in **frame** to **fl** to spell another word for **fire**.

   _____

7. Make another new word by changing the **c** in **came** to **t**.

   _____

8. Write a sentence to tell what the new word means.

   _____

   _____

Macmillan/McGraw-Hill

8

Level 4/Unit 2
Challenge Extension: Have children practice the words *just* and *home* by completing the
following sentences: "I *just* finished _____ . When I go *home,* I like to _____ ."

93

/ā/-ame

Finding Mistakes

Read Jill's story. Circle the six mistakes she made.
Write the correct words on the lines.

My brother Luke cume to the gam with a girl named
sarah. She is the sime girl he took to tha school
dance. He keeps her picture in a fame on his desk.

1. _____	2. _____
3. _____	4. _____
5. _____	6. _____

Writing Activity

Write two sentences about a game you like.

_____

_____

_____

/ā/-ame

Write the spelling word for each sentence.
Remember that all the words in this pattern rhyme
with **tame**.

1. It begins like . _____

2. It begins like  . _____

3. It begins like  . _____

4. It begins like  . _____

5. The word that spells  is _____ .

Fix the mixed-up letters to make spelling words.

6. mena _____   7. esma _____

8. meac _____   9. amfer _____

10. agem _____

Macmillan/McGraw-Hill

/ō/ -old

Pretest Directions
Fold back the paper in half. Use the blanks to write each word as it is read aloud. When you finish the test, unfold the paper. Use the list at the left to correct any spelling mistakes. Practice the words you missed for the Final Test.

To Parents
Here are the results of your child's weekly spelling Pretest. You can help your child study for the Final Test by following these simple steps for each word on the list:

1. Read the word to your child.

2. Have your child write the word, saying each letter as it is written.

3. Say each letter of the word as your child checks the spelling.

4. If a mistake has been made, have your child read each letter of the correctly spelled word aloud and then repeat steps 1–3.

Parent/Child Activity
Help your child to use each of the new words in sentences about the family.

1. old
2. gold
3. told
4. sold
5. cold

1. _____
2. _____
3. _____
4. _____
5. _____

Challenge Words
him

new

Challenge Words
_____

_____

/ō/-old

1. All of the spelling words end with the three
letters _____, _____, _____.

2. Write the spelling words that have four letters.

_____   _____

_____   _____

Fix these spelling words by adding the missing letters.

3. s_____ld   **4.** to_____

5. go_____   **6.** c_____

Write three new words by adding **b, f,** and **h** to **old**.

7. _____   **8.** _____

9. _____

/ō/-old

Read the sentences. Write the spelling words that
are missing.

The grocer _____ fresh eggs. He kept
the eggs in a _____ place. Someone
_____ my mother that his eggs were
too _____ to buy. The grocer told her
that they were as good as _____.

Some of the spelling words tell about things that
happened before now. Write the missing word.

1. My dad tells me a story every night. Last night he
_____ about meeting a bear.

2. In the summer, my sister and I sell lemonade. Last
summer we _____ a lot of lemonade.

3. Which word means "not new"? _____

Challenge Extension: Have children draw pictures to illustrate
the words *him* and *new*. Ask children to label their pictures.

Level 4/Unit 2   **8**

Macmillan/McGraw-Hill

/ō/-old

Finding Mistakes

Jamika can tell a good story, but she has trouble with her writing. Help her fix her report. Circle the mistakes. Write the words as they should be.

A store near home suld old golde bracelets. i showed them to my Aunt bea. One day when i was home with a cole, she came to se mi. She gave me a new charm on a chain. Surprise!

1. _____ 2. _____

3. _____ 4. _____

5. _____ 6. _____

7. _____ 8. _____

Writing Activity

Write sentences about something made of gold. Use two spelling words.

_____

_____

_____

_____

/ō/-old

Use these clues to write the spelling words.

1. The word that begins like  is

_____.

2. The word that begins like  is

_____.

3. The word that begins like  is

_____.

4. The word that begins like is

_____.

5. The word that begins with the sound you hear

in  is _____.

Find the spelling words
in the puzzle.
Circle the words.
One is on a slant.

```
g  s  m  o  l  t
t  o  l  d  e  l
l  l  l  g  o  o
e  d  s  d  l  c
b  c  o  l  d  o
```

/ī/-*ide*

Pretest Directions
Fold back the paper in half. Use the blanks to write each word as it is read aloud. When you finish the test, unfold the paper. Use the list at the right to correct any spelling mistakes. Practice the words you missed for the Final Test.

To Parents
Here are the results of your child's weekly spelling Pretest. You can help your child study for the Final Test by following these simple steps for each word on the list:

1. Read the word to your child.

2. Have your child write the word, saying each letter as it is written.

3. Say each letter of the word as your child checks the spelling.

4. If a mistake has been made, have your child read each letter of the correctly spelled word aloud and then repeat steps 1–3.

Parent/Child Activity
Ask your child to find examples of this pattern in a familiar book.

1. _____   **1.** side

2. _____   **2.** wide

3. _____   **3.** slide

4. _____   **4.** ride

5. _____   **5.** hide

Challenge Words   **Challenge Words**

_____   first

_____   find

Macmillan/McGraw-Hill

/ī/-*ide*

Add **e** to each word to make spelling words.

1. hid   _____

2. slid   _____

3. rid   _____

Circle the pairs that rhyme. Write the rhyming word pairs.

wide	hid	slime	road	ride
slide	hide	slide	ride	hide

4. _____   _____

5. _____   _____

6. Write a new word by changing the **w** of **wide** to **sl**.

_____

Macmillan/McGraw-Hill

/ī/-ide

Fill in the missing letters in the poem. Use the letters **ide**.

Bes_____ the sea, we watched the t_____.

The waves rolled in both high and w_____.

Ins_____ a cave, the small fish h_____.

They miss the otter as he fishes.

The otter finds small fish delicious.

5

Level 4/Unit 2

Challenge Extension: Have children practice the words *first* and *find* by writing complete sentences that answer the following questions: "What is your *first* name? Where can you *find* lots of books?"

103

/ī/ -ide

Finding Mistakes

The class wrote silly sentences,
but they made some mistakes.
Circle their mistakes.
Write the words correctly.

Tha elephant's bike was too wid for me to ride.

1. _____   **2.** _____

The old cat creeps beside the slid to hie.

3. _____   **4.** _____

the mouse liks to skate inside.

5. _____   **6.** _____

Writing Activity

Write a sentence about playing outside. Use two spelling
words in it.

_____

_____

/ī/-ide

Write the missing letters for each spelling word.

1. s _____ _____ _____

2. r _____ d _____

3. s l _____ _____ _____

4. w _____ _____ _____

5. h _____ _____ _____

Put the spelling words into the boxes to complete the puzzle.

Across

  3. to travel in or on something

  5. to slip down or around

Down

  1. to go where you can't be seen

  2. not thin

  4. an edge

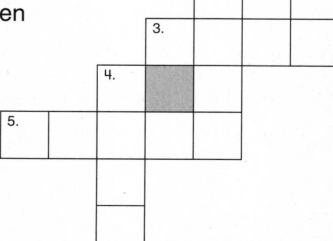

/ā/-ay

Pretest Directions
Fold back the paper in half. Use the blanks to write each word as it is read aloud. When you finish the test, unfold the paper. Use the list at the left to correct any spelling mistakes. Practice the words you missed for the Final Test.

To Parents
Here are the results of your child's weekly spelling Pretest. You can help your child study for the Final Test by following these simple steps for each word on the list:

1. Read the word to your child.

2. Have your child write the word, saying each letter as it is written.

3. Say each letter of the word as your child checks the spelling.

4. If a mistake has been made, have your child read each letter of the correctly spelled word aloud and then repeat steps 1–3.

Parent/Child Activity
Ask your child to tell you the two letters that are the same in each word.

1. away

2. anyway

3. bay

4. day

5. say

1. _____

2. _____

3. _____

4. _____

5. _____

Challenge Words

every

only

Challenge Words

_____

_____

/ā/ -ay

Write the rest of the spelling words so they are in ABC order. Circle the two letters that are in every word.

1. anyway

2. _____

3. _____

4. _____

5. _____

Circle the spelling word in these longer words.

6. birthday   **7.** weekday   **8.** holiday

9. Monday   **10.** bayberry   **11.** Wednesday

12. saying   **13.** Friday

Change the **b** of **bay** to **pl**, **gr**, and **tr** to make new words. Write the words.

14. _____   **15.** _____   **16.** _____

/ā/-ay

Write the correct spelling word on the line.

1. Which word means a body of water?

_____

2. Friday is the name of a _____.

3. Which word means "to speak"?_____

4. Which word means "in another place"?

_____

5. Which word means "whatever" or "anyhow"?

_____

Write a spelling word that means the opposite of each word below.

6. night   _____

7. near   _____

8. be silent   _____

Word Journal

Write all the days of the week in your Word Journal.

Challenge Extension: Have children practice the words *every* and *only* by completing the following sentences: "*Every* day I_____. I have *only* one_____."

/ā/ -ay

Finding Mistakes

Adam wrote to his family while he was at camp. He made some mistakes. Circle them and write the words correctly.

Dear mom, dad, and becky,

I must say that I like to play all daye here. we swim in the bay and i am learning to canoe. I took A picture of my friends swimming in the bay. I feel far eway from you. Anway, I will came home next week.

1. _____ 2. _____

3. _____ 4. _____

5. _____ 6. _____

7. _____ 8. _____

9. _____ 10. _____

Writing Activity

Have you ever been away from home? What did you do? How did you feel? Write two sentences about being away from home. Use two of your spelling words.

_____

_____

_____

/āl-ay

Write a spelling word to complete each sentence.

1. My friend lives far _____.

2. The boat floats in the _____.

3. I used to nap every _____.

4. What did you _____?

5. Sometimes I'm wrong, but I always

   try _____.

Fix the mixed-up letters to make spelling words.

6. yad   _____

7. yas   _____

8. aby   _____

9. nawyya   _____

10. wyaa   _____

/ā/-ace

Pretest Directions
Fold the paper in half. Use the blanks to write each word as it is read aloud. When you finish the test, unfold the paper. Use the list on the right to correct any spelling mistakes. Practice the words you missed for the Final Test.

To Parents
Here are the results of your child's weekly spelling Pretest. You can help your child study for the Final Test by following these simple steps for each word on the list:

1. Read the word to your child.

2. Have your child write the word, saying each letter as it is written.

3. Say each letter of the word as your child checks the spelling.

4. If a mistake has been made, have your child read each letter of the correctly spelled word aloud and then repeat steps 1–3.

Parent/Child Activity
Ask your child to make up sentences using some of the new words.

1. _____

2. _____

3. _____

4. _____

5. _____

1. place

2. space

3. face

4. race

5. trace

Challenge Words

_____

_____

Challenge Words

have

work

/ā/-ace

Complete each of the spelling words.

1. pl _____

2. sp _____

3. tr _____

4. r _____

5. f _____

Unscramble each word. Write the words on the lines.

6. ecapl _____

7. acer _____

8. afce _____

9. acesp _____

10. etrac _____

/ā/-ace

Write the word that makes sense in each sentence.

1. The children ran in a _____ .

2. There was only a _____ of snow
on the hill.

3. The coats took up all the _____ in
the closet.

4. The table is the _____ for the big
vase.

5. Eric had a funny look on his _____.

Level 5, Unit 1
Challenge Extension: Have children write one or two sentences, using the
words *have* and *work*. Children may wish to illustrate their sentences.

113

Macmillan/McGraw-Hill

/ā/-ace

Finding Mistakes

Circle the word in each sentence that does not make sense. Write the correct word on the line.

1. There is no race left. _____

2. The eyes on that space are very large. _____

3. My trace is at the first table. _____

4. Hamilton won the second face. _____

5. To draw over a line is to race it. _____

Word Journal

The spelling pattern **ace** is a word by itself. Add **gr, br,** and **l** to **ace**.

6. _____

7. _____

8. _____

Macmillan/McGraw-Hill

/ā/ -ace

Put your spelling words in ABC order. The first one is done for you.

1. face

2. _____

3. _____

4. _____

5. _____

Choose spelling words to complete the rhymes.

6. This is a good _____

to run a _____.

7. I used a pencil to _____

the picture of the boy's _____.

/ū/ -use

Pretest Directions
Fold the paper in half. Use the blanks to write each word as it is read aloud. When you finish the test, unfold the paper. Use the list on the left to correct any spelling mistakes. Practice the words you missed for the Final Test.

To Parents
Here are the results of your child's weekly spelling Pretest. You can help your child study for the Final Test by following these simple steps for each word on the list:

1. Read the word to your child.

2. Have your child write the word, saying each letter as it is written.

3. Say each letter of the word as your child checks the spelling.

4. If a mistake has been made, have your child read each letter of the correctly spelled word aloud and then repeat steps 1–3.

Parent/Child Activity
Help your child make up a story using at least three of the spelling words.

1. use
2. amuse
3. refuse
4. fuse
5. confuse

1. _____
2. _____
3. _____
4. _____
5. _____

Challenge Words

would

could

Challenge Words

_____

_____

/ū/-use

The kites can only catch the wind when the words are spelled correctly.

Fix the words and write them on the lines.

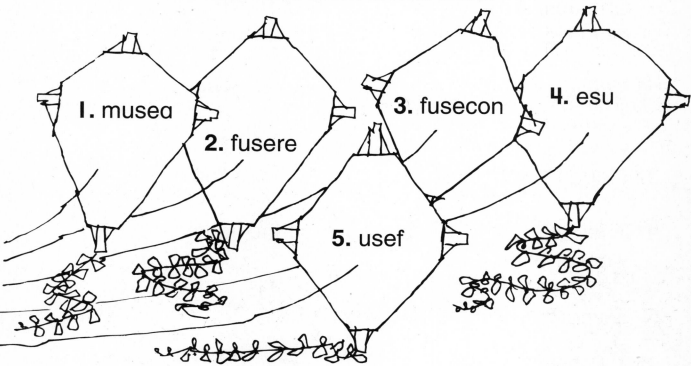

1. musea

2. fusere

3. fusecon

4. esu

5. usef

Then circle the three letters that are the same in all the words.

1. _____   **2.** _____

3. _____   **4.** _____

5. _____

/ū/-use

Write the spelling word that belongs in each sentence. Some words are used two times.

I. Christa likes to _____ red paint in her pictures.

2. She would _____ to use green paint.

3. I laugh when jokes _____ me.

4. The _____ blew out, so the lights would not go on.

5. Sentences with hard words can _____ me.

6. Did his funny trick _____ you?

7. You can _____ this pencil to draw.

8. Don't let the map _____ you.

Challenge Extension: Give children practice with the words *would* and *could* by having them write the answers to the following questions: "What *would* you do if a monkey came to your house to play with you? How *could* you make your neighborhood a better place in which to live?"

Macmillan/McGraw-Hill

/ū/-use

Finding Mistakes

Find the five mistakes in the story and circle them. Then write the correction on the line.

last night, the lights went out in our family room. mom said it was a fus. my little brother began to cry. I tried to amuze him while Mom went to fix it.

1. _____   2. _____

3. _____   4. _____

5. _____

Writing Activity

Have the lights ever gone out in your house? Tell what happened or make up a story about what might have happened. Use three spelling words.

_____

_____

_____

_____

/ū/-use

Complete the spelling words. Then they will be in ABC order.

1. a_____ **2.** c_____

3. f_____ **4.** r_____

5. u_____

Pictures Can Tell Stories

Look at these children. Which one is amused? Which one is confused? Which one is refusing something?

Write the spelling word that belongs with each picture.

6.

7.

8.

6. _____ **7.** _____

8. _____

/ī/-ine

Pretest Directions
Fold the paper in half. Use the blanks to write each word as it is read aloud. When you finish the test, unfold the paper. Use the list on the right to correct any spelling mistakes. Practice the words you missed for the Final Test.

To Parents
Here are the results of your child's weekly spelling Pretest. You can help your child study for the Final Test by following these simple steps for each word on the list:

1. Read the word to your child.

2. Have your child write the word, saying each letter as it is written.

3. Say each letter of the word as your child checks the spelling.

4. If a mistake has been made, have your child read each letter of the correctly spelled word aloud and then repeat steps 1–3.

Parent/Child Activity
Play a rhyming game with your child. Take turns saying and writing words that rhyme with "fine."

1. _____
2. _____
3. _____
4. _____
5. _____

1. mine
2. fine
3. shine
4. line
5. nine

Challenge Words

_____

_____

Challenge Words

back

around

/ī/ -ine

1. Write the spelling word that has five letters.

_____

2. Write the word that tells how many stars.

_____

Write a spelling word that begins like each of the pictures.

3.  _____

4.  _____

5.  _____

Now go back to the words you wrote. Circle the letters that are the same in each word.

/ī/-ine

Write the spelling word that makes sense in each sentence.

1. That toy is yours, but this one is _____.

2. I hope the sun will _____ today.

3. Use this pencil to draw a _____.

4. Eight plus one makes _____.

5. Today I really feel _____!

6. We get in_____ to buy lunch.

7. Use the brush to _____ your shoes.

8. We dig gold from a _____ in the ground.

Macmillan/McGraw-Hill

Level 5, Unit 1
Challenge Extension: Give children oral practice with the words *back* and *around*. Have them talk about something that is in *back* of the classroom. Then, have them walk *around* a specific object in the classroom. Have them say complete sentences, using each word.

8

/ī/-*ine*

Finding Mistakes

Read the story. Circle the words that are wrong.
Write them the right way on the lines.

My brother and I woke up at nime. I felt fin. We had plans.
mine were for a picnic, but the sun refused to shin. Dark
clouds raced in a line across the sky. It began to rain. our
picnic would be another tim.

1. _____   2. _____

3. _____   4. _____

5. _____   6. _____

Word Puzzles

Write the new words you can make.

7. **sw + ine** = _____

8. **tw + ine** = _____

9. **sp + ine** = _____

10. **wh + ine** = _____

11. **p + ine** = _____

12. **d + ine** = _____

Macmillan/McGraw-Hill

/ī/ -*ine*

Write the five spelling words in ABC order.

1. _____ 2._____

3. _____ 4._____

5. _____

Circle the spelling word in each pair. Then write it on the line.

fine	mine	name
fun	main	nine
shone	line	
shine	lane	

6. _____ 7._____

8. _____ 9._____

10. _____

/ī/ -ight

Pretest Directions
Fold back the paper in half. Use the blanks to write each word as it is read aloud. When you finish the test, unfold the paper. Use the list on the left to correct any spelling mistakes. Practice the words you missed for the Final Test.

To Parents
Here are the results of your child's weekly spelling Pretest. You can help your child study for the Final Test by following these simple steps for each word on the list:

1. Read the word to your child.

2. Have your child write the word, saying each letter as it is written.

3. Say each letter of the word as your child checks the spelling.

4. If a mistake has been made, have your child read each letter of the correctly spelled word aloud and then repeat steps 1–3.

Parent/Child Activity
With your child, make up a rhyme about night, using words with the **ight** pattern.

1. night	**1.** _____
2. fight	**2.** _____
3. bright	**3.** _____
4. might	**4.** _____
5. sight	**5.** _____

Challenge Words

next

they

Challenge Words

_____

_____

/ī/ -*ight*

Choose the correct spelling word for each sentence.
Then circle the letters that are the same in each word.

1. The opposite of **day** is _____.

2. If you see well, you have good _____.

3. When the sun shines, the day is _____.

4. Bad feelings can lead to a _____.

5. Another word for **may** is _____.

Word Puzzles

Write the new words you can make.

6. fl + **ight** = _____

7. kn + **ight** = _____

8. l + **ight** = _____

Macmillan/McGraw-Hill

/ī/ -ight

Write the spelling word that makes the best sense
in each sentence.

1. Good new shoes _____ last a
whole year.

2. In one fairy story, twelve princesses danced all

_____.

3. By morning, their slippers looked dull, not

_____.

4. "Our shoes look as if we were in a

_____."

5. One princess cried, "What a _____!"

Add **ight** to complete the missing word.

6. The king, their father, was in a fr_____.

Add a spelling word to make a new word.

7. "The stars look very bright to _____."

Write a spelling word.

8. Make a wish with all your _____.

Macmillan/McGraw-Hill

Level 5, Unit 1

8

Challenge Extension: Give children oral practice with the words *next* and *they* by having them answer
questions that you make up; for example, "Where are the crayons?" Children must answer, using the
word *they*. "What would you like to do *next*?" Children must answer, using the word *next*.

/ī/ -*ight*

Finding Mistakes

Read the story. Circle all the spelling words that are spelled wrong. Then write them correctly on the lines.

The sit of our messy room made my sister want to fght. "It mite take all nigh to clean up," she cried. "I'll make it clean and ightbr, I said. "And I'll do it right away."

1. _____ 2. _____

3. _____ 4. _____

5. _____

Writing Activity

Read this poem.

Star light, star bright,
First star I see tonight.
Wish I may, wish I might
Have the wish I wish tonight.

Make a wish. Write about it using two spelling words.

_____

_____

_____

/ī/ -*ight*

Complete the words in the list.

1. br_____

2. f_____

3. m_____

4. n_____

5. s_____

Fill in the blanks with spelling words.

1. not day, but _____

2. not dull, but _____

3. not sound, but _____

4. not play, but _____

5. not must, but _____

Level 5, Unit 1   10

/ou/-own

Pretest Directions
Fold back the paper in half. Use the blanks to write each word as it is read aloud. When you finish the test, unfold the paper. Use the list on the right to correct any spelling mistakes. Practice the words you missed for the Final Test.

To Parents
Here are the results of your child's weekly spelling Pretest. You can help your child study for the Final Test by following these simple steps for each word on the list:

1. Read the word to your child.

2. Have your child write the word, saying each letter as it is written.

3. Say each letter of the word as your child checks the spelling.

4. If a mistake has been made, have your child read each letter of the correctly spelled word aloud and then repeat steps 1–3.

Parent/Child Activity
Talk with your child about clowns— the colors they wear, and the expressions on their faces. Ask your child to write a sentence about them.

1. _____
2. _____
3. _____
4. _____
5. _____

1. down
2. brown
3. town
4. clown
5. frown

Challenge Words

_____

_____

Challenge Words

were

/ou/-own

Write each word. Then circle the letters that are the same in each word.

1. Write the word that names a color.

_____

2. Write the word that would come last in ABC
order. _____

3. Write the word for 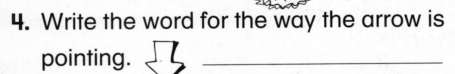 . _____

4. Write the word for the way the arrow is
pointing. _____

5. Write the word that begins with **fr**.

_____

Write the missing letters to complete each spelling
word.

6. br _____   **7. cl** _____

8. t _____   **9. fr** _____

10. d _____

/ou/-*own*

Write the spelling word that goes on the line.

Across

2. A small city is called a _____.

4. In the fall, leaves turn red and yellow and then

_____.

5. A funny person in the circus is a _____.

Down

1. Which word is the opposite of **smile**? _____

3. Which word is the opposite of **up**? _____

Write the answers in the puzzle.

Macmillan/McGraw-Hill

10 Level 5, Unit 2
Challenge Extension: To give children practice with the word *off*, have them draw pictures of three
things that can be turned on and *off*. Have them label pictures with the word *off*.

133

/ou/ -own

Finding Mistakes

Circle the mistakes below. Write the
words correctly on the lines.

The tired old clow

in green and bron

wore a frown.

as he gently sat down,

he said, "i wish

we could leave this ton."

1. _____

2. _____

3. _____

4. _____

5. _____

Writing Activity

Have you ever seen a clown in a circus or on TV?
Write a sentence to tell what the clown did. Use two
of your spelling words.

_____

_____

_____

/ou/-*own*

Complete each word.

1. fr _____

2. cl _____

3. t _____

4. d _____

5. br _____

Help the mouse escape from the cat.

Write the correct spelling on each line to lead the mouse to its little home.

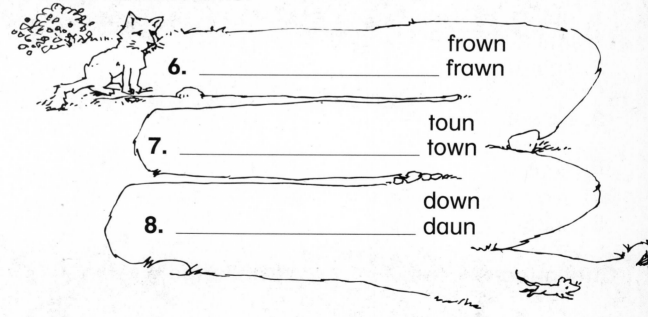

6. _____   frown
frawn

7. _____   toun
town

8. _____   down
daun

9. _____   klown   clown

10. _____   brown   brow

/ou/-out

Pretest Directions

Fold back the paper in half. Use the blanks to write each word as it is read aloud. When you finish the test, unfold the paper. Use the list on the left to correct any spelling mistakes. Practice the words you missed for the Final Test.

To Parents

Here are the results of your child's weekly spelling Pretest. You can help your child study for the Final Test by following these simple steps for each word on the list:

1. Read the word to your child.

2. Have your child write the word, saying each letter as it is written.

3. Say each letter of the word as your child checks the spelling.

4. If a mistake has been made, have your child read each letter of the correctly spelled word aloud and then repeat steps 1–3.

Parent/Child Activity

Help your child to sprout a bean on a damp paper towel and print a label: *bean sprout*.

1. out

2. shout

3. sprout

4. pout

5. scout

1. _____

2. _____

3. _____

4. _____

5. _____

Challenge Words

our

house

Challenge Words

_____

_____

/ou/-out

Fill the cups! Use the letters
sh, spr, sc, and **p** to complete
the spelling words.

out

sh
spr
sc
p

_____ **out**

_____ **out**

_____ **out**

_____ **out**

Write the spelling word that is in all the
other spelling words. _____

/ou/-out

Complete each sentence with a spelling word.

1. When a seed starts to grow, it becomes a

_____.

2. Please speak more softly. You must not

_____.

3. Someone who can follow a trail in the woods

is a _____.

4. The opposite of **in** is _____.

5. If you don't get your way, you should not

_____.

Word Journal

6. Change the letters **sh** in **shout** to **tr** to write a

word for a kind of fish. _____

Macmillan/McGraw-Hill

Challenge Extension: Have children write a short story that uses the words *our* and *house*. The story can be real or make-believe.

/ou/ -out

Finding Mistakes

Maria was in a hurry when she wrote in her journal. Find her mistakes. Write the words correctly on the lines.

I went to my skout meeting. We played tag. Then Jan called, "Time owt! i lost my ring."

We helped her look for it. then we heard a shoute. Terry had found the ring.

1. _____   2. _____

3. _____   4. _____

5. _____

Writing Activity

Write a sentence about growing a seed. Use two spelling words.

_____

_____

/ou/-out

1. Write the spelling word that begins with the same sound as **pan**. _____

2. Write the spelling word that begins with the same sound as **scamp**. _____

3. Write the spelling word that begins with the same sound as **shut**. _____

4. Write the spelling word that begins with the same sound as **spring**. _____

5. Write the spelling word that you find in all the other spelling words. _____

Find and circle the spelling words in the puzzle.

o	u	t	s	p	u
t	r	s	c	o	p
s	p	r	o	u	t
s	h	o	u	t	o
s	r	o	t	u	t

Macmillan/McGraw-Hill

/ou/-ound

Pretest Directions
Fold back the paper in half. Use the blanks to write each word as it is read aloud. When you finish the test, unfold the paper. Use the list on the right to correct any spelling mistakes. Practice the words you missed for the Final Test.

To Parents
Here are the results of your child's weekly spelling Pretest. You can help your child study for the Final Test by following these simple steps for each word on the list:

1. Read the word to your child.

2. Have your child write the word, saying each letter as it is written.

3. Say each letter of the word as your child checks the spelling.

4. If a mistake has been made, have your child read each letter of the correctly spelled word aloud and then repeat steps 1–3.

Parent/Child Activity
Make up silly rhymes with your child and use the spelling pattern for a drumming beat.

1. _____

2. _____

3. _____

4. _____

5. _____

1. sound

2. ground

3. pound

4. round

5. hound

Challenge Words

_____

_____

Challenge Words

don't

well

/ou/-*ound*

All of the new spelling words end with the letters **ound**.
Write the letters that complete the spelling words.

1. _____ **p**

2. _____ **gr**

3. _____ **h**

4. _____ **r**

5. _____ **s**

Read the sentences. Find three new words that
have the letters **ound**. Write the words on the lines.

I rode around on the merry-go-round. Happy music
played in the background.

6. _____

7. _____

8. _____

/ou/ -ound

Write the spelling words to complete each sentence.

1. A _____ is a kind of dog.

2. He was not quiet. He made a

_____.

3. The opposite of **flat** is _____.

4. The cake weighs one _____.

5. The earth we walk on is our

_____.

Circle the word pairs that rhyme.

On the lines, write the word pairs that rhyme.

sound	**round**	**ground**	**hound**	**pound**
bound	**rind**	**grind**	**sound**	**round**

6. _____

7. _____

8. _____

8

Level 5, Unit 2

Challenge Extension: Have children make up one or two funny book titles that use the words *don't* and *well*. Children may want to design a book cover to go with each title.

143

Macmillan/McGraw-Hill

/ou/-*ound*

Finding Mistakes

Find and circle six mistakes in the story.
Write the words correctly on the lines.

   the old brown hound hid on the grownd below
the shed. The sond of his loud howling woke
Grandfather. He found his cane and rand out to
chase the poor dog away. grandfather shouted as
He and the dog ran round and round the shed.

1. _____

2. _____

3. _____

4. _____

5. _____

6. _____

Macmillan/McGraw-Hill

/ou/-ound

Write the spelling words in the boxes to complete the puzzle. Use the clues.

Across

3. like a ball

4. to hit with a hammer

5. a kind of dog

Down

1. something you hear

2. It is under your feet.

Write new words by changing the **h** of **hound** to **b**, and to **w**, and then to **m**.

1. _____

2. _____

3. _____

Macmillan/McGraw-Hill

/ā/ -ail

Pretest Directions
Fold back the paper in half. Use the blanks to write each word as it is read aloud. When you finish the test, unfold the paper. Use the list on the left to correct any spelling mistakes. Practice the words you missed for the Final Test.

To Parents,
Here are the results of your child's weekly spelling Pretest. You can help your child study for the Final Test by following these simple steps for each word on the list:

1. Read the word to your child.

2. Have your child write the word, saying each letter as it is written.

3. Say each letter of the word as your child checks the spelling.

4. If a mistake has been made, have your child read each letter of the correctly spelled word aloud and then repeat steps 1–3.

Parent/Child Activity
Help your child to write a party invitation or a thank-you letter. Address it, stamp it, and mail it.

1. mail
2. sail
3. pail
4. nail
5. trail

1. _____
2. _____
3. _____
4. _____
5. _____

Challenge Words

ask

come

Challenge Words

_____

_____

/ā/-ail

Long ago, farm fences had steps to climb over. See how fast you can climb the steps over this fence. Write the letters to complete the spelling word on each step.

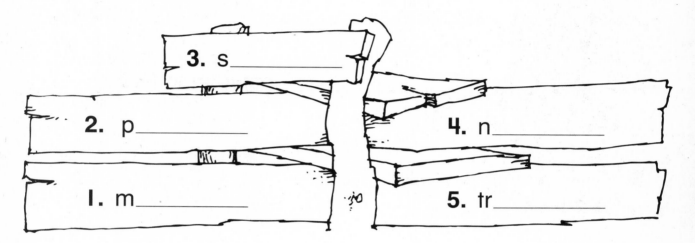

3. s_____

2. p_____

4. n_____

1. m_____

5. tr_____

Word Puzzles

Many words you know are spelled with the **ail** pattern. Subtract and add beginning letters to make new words.

6. **mail – m + r =** _____

7. **trail – tr + fr =** _____

8. **pail – p + t =** _____

/ā/-ail

Choose the right spelling word to complete each sentence.

1. You need a stamp to _____ a letter.

2. It took a _____ of water to fill the birdbath.

3. The scout could follow the _____ of the deer.

4. You need a good wind to _____ on the lake.

5. He hit the _____ with the hammer.

Write three spelling words to finish the rhyme.

I'll put away my shovel and _____,

Take out my boat and go for a _____.

I'll write you a letter from far away.

It will be in the _____ the very next day.

Challenge Extension: Have children write and design a party invitation that uses the words *ask* and *come*. Children may exchange invitations with their classmates.

8

Macmillan/McGraw-Hill

/ā/-ail

Finding Mistakes

Circle the mistakes in the story.

Write the words correctly on the lines.

Billy wanted to carry the mail home from the post office. it was a stormy day. A great wind caught the letters. It made them sale out over the street. billy followed the trail of the flying letters. Then he found an old pil. Now he could carry his mail safely home.

1. _____

2. _____

3. _____

4. _____

Writing Activity

Write a letter to a friend. Tell about things you did at the beach. Use two spelling words.

_____

_____

_____

_____

/ā/ -ail

Write a spelling word for each picture.

1. _____

2. _____

3. _____

4. _____

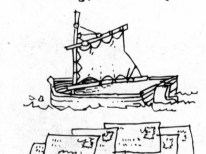

5. _____

Add the spelling words to complete each sentence.

I walked down the _____ to get

the _____.

I carried it home in my silver _____.

Handwriting Hints

Steps to Follow

1. Sit in a natural, easy way.
2. Sit up straight.
3. Hold your pencil lightly, but firmly.
4. Place your paper correctly.

Self-Check Questions

✓ Is my handwriting smooth?

✓ Are my letters evenly spaced?

✓ Are my words evenly spaced?

✓ Are my letters shaped correctly?

✓ Are my letters the correct size?

✓ Do all of my letters sit on the baseline?

✓ Do my capital letters touch the top line?

✓ Do all of my letters slant in the same direction?

Handwriting Guidelines

SMOOTHNESS
Make each letter smooth and clear.

please

thank you

SPACING
Space each letter evenly. Where the last letter in a word ends, the next one begins.

Hello!

SHAPE
Make each letter the correct shape.

I like you.

Make each letter the correct size.

Do you like me?

Make each letter touch the lines correctly.

robot

radio

Handwriting Models

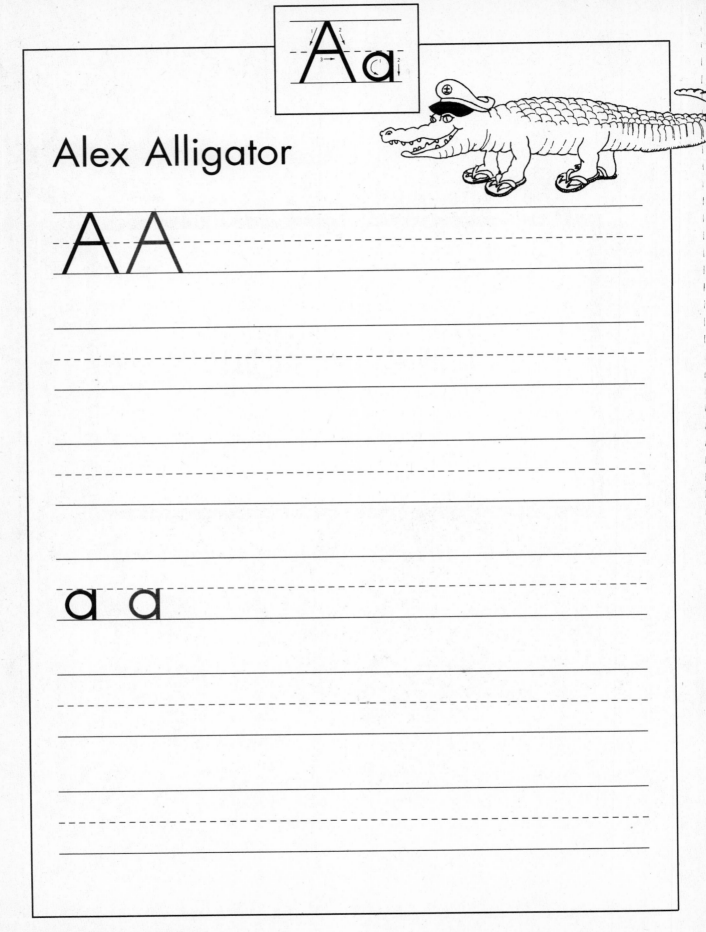

Alex Alligator

A A

a a

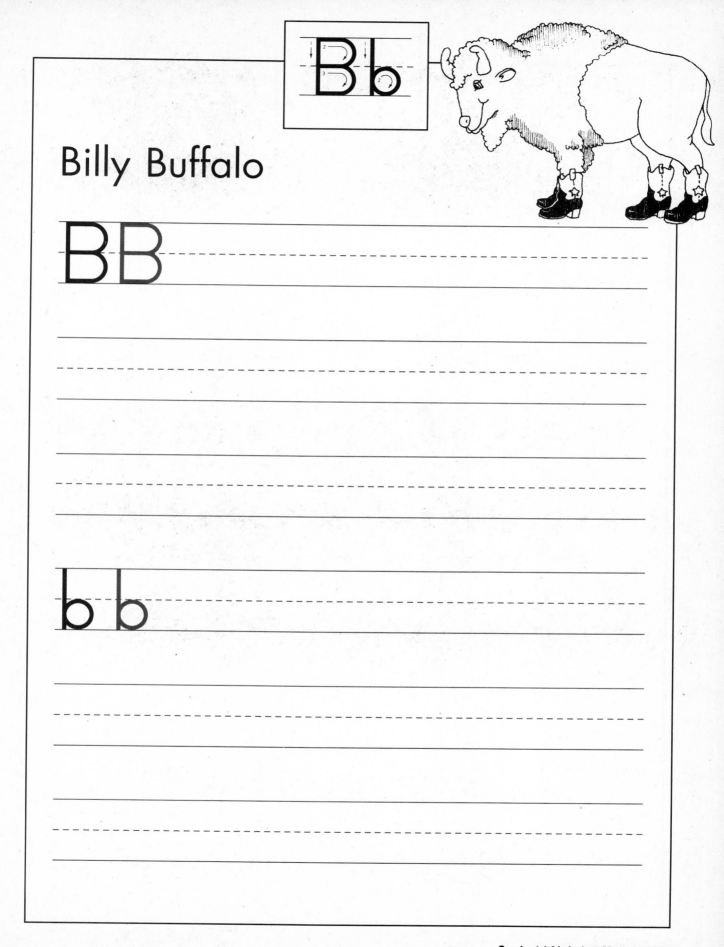

Billy Buffalo

BB

bb

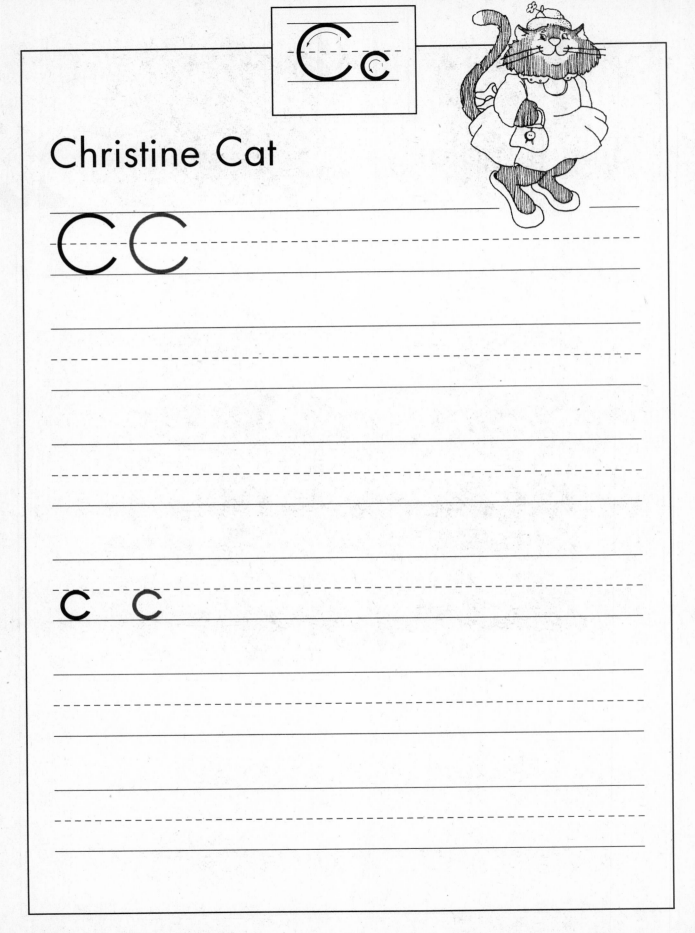

Christine Cat

C C

C C

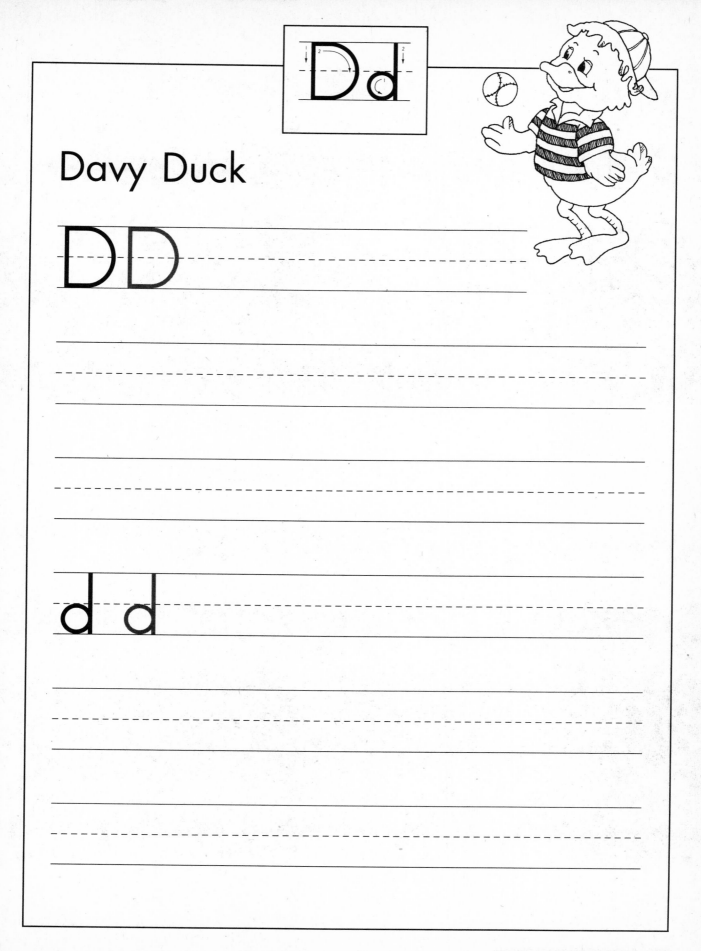

Davy Duck

D D

d d

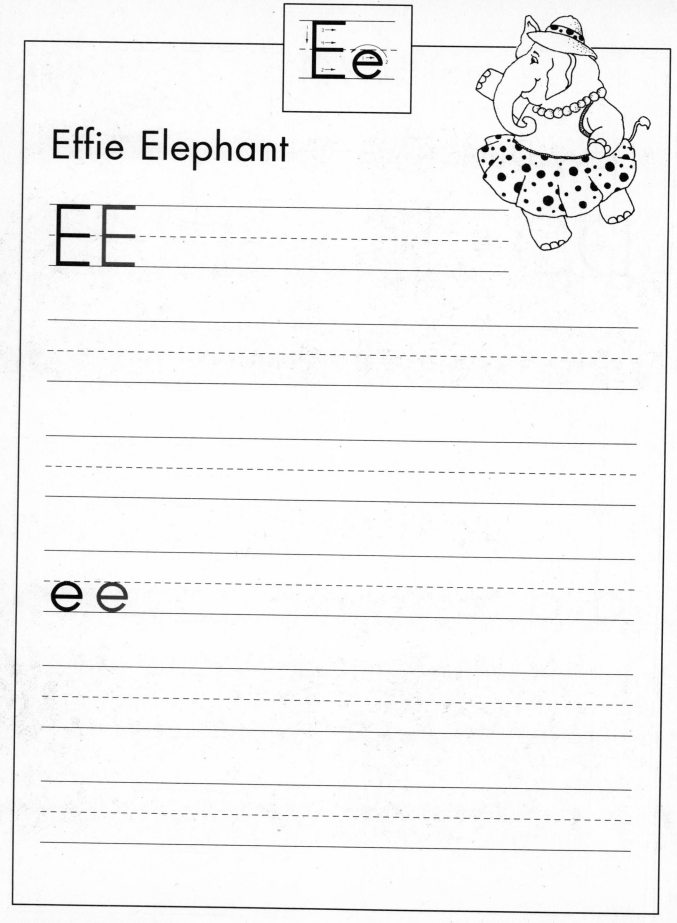

Effie Elephant

E E

e e

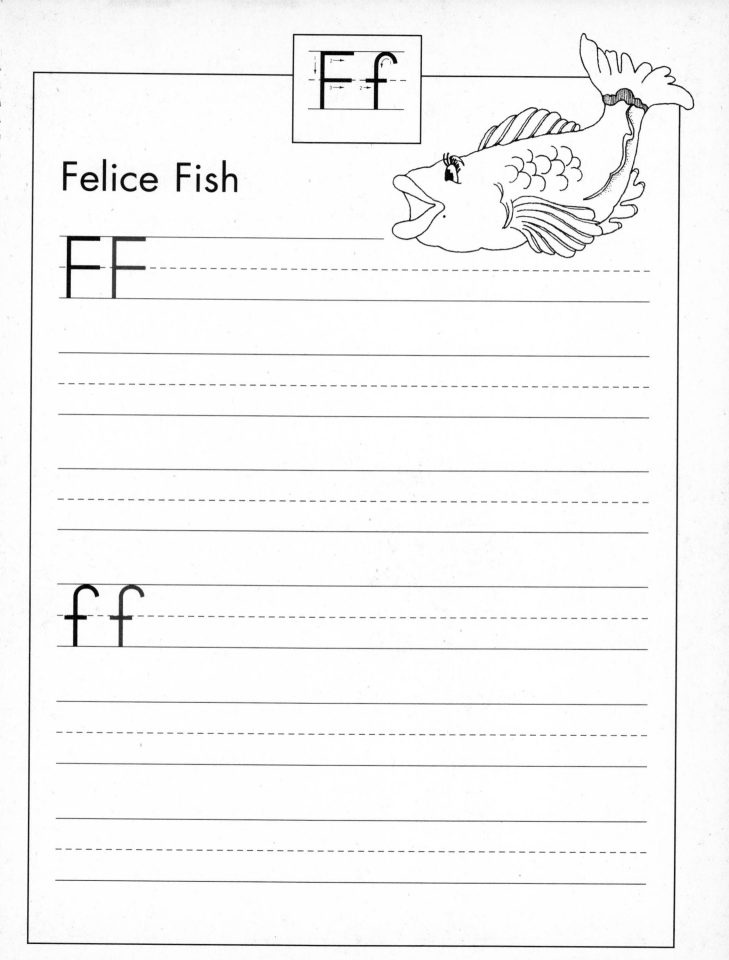

Felice Fish

F F

f f

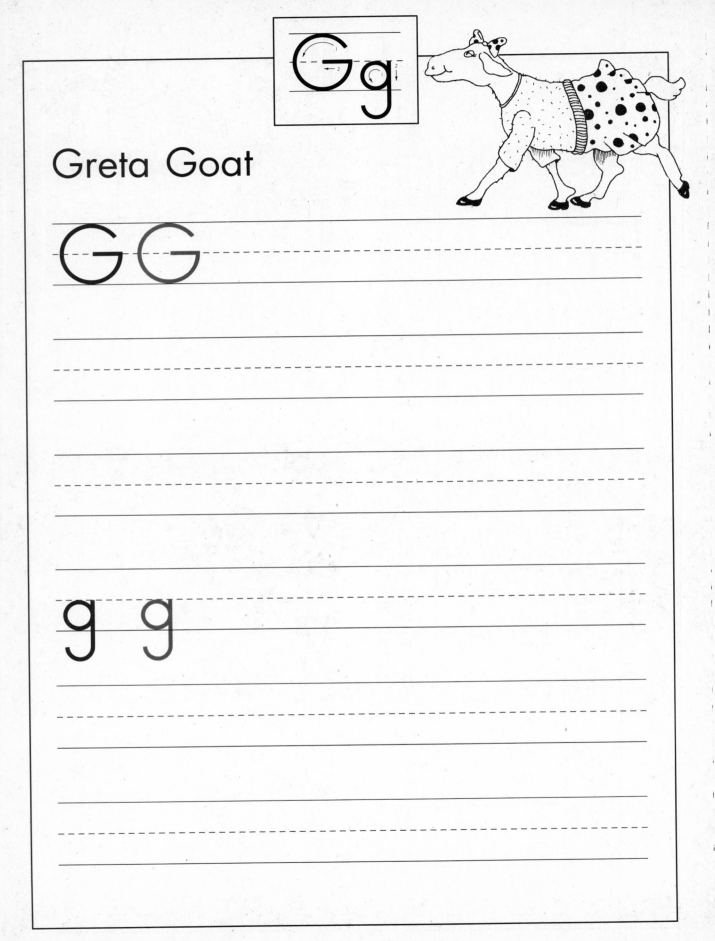

Greta Goat

G G

g g

Heddy Horse

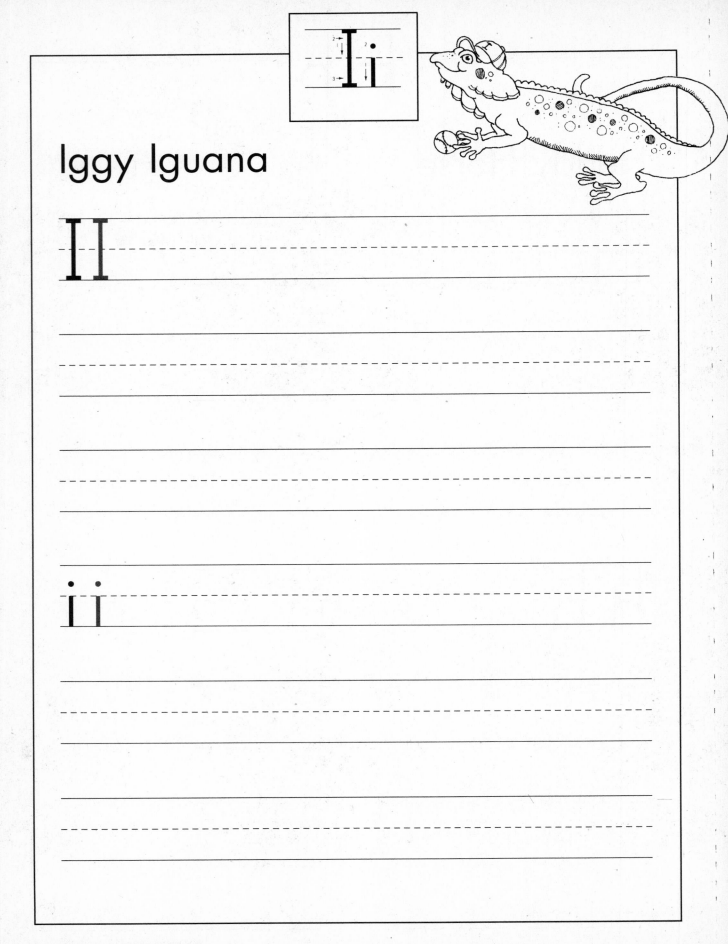

Iggy Iguana

I I

i i

Jackie Jaguar

J J

j j

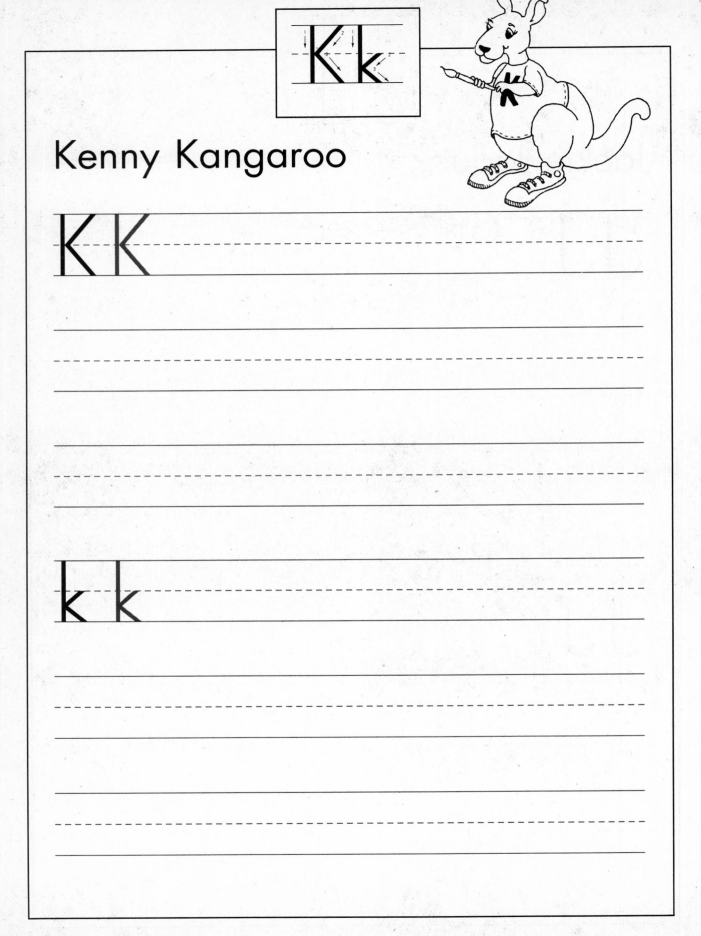

Kenny Kangaroo

K K

k k

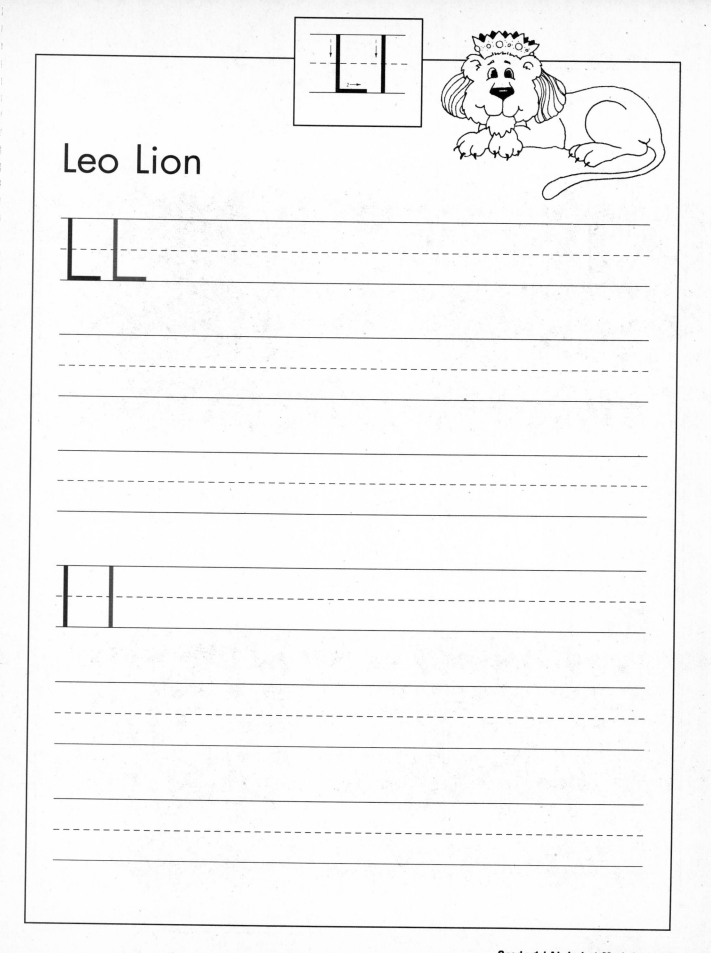

Leo Lion

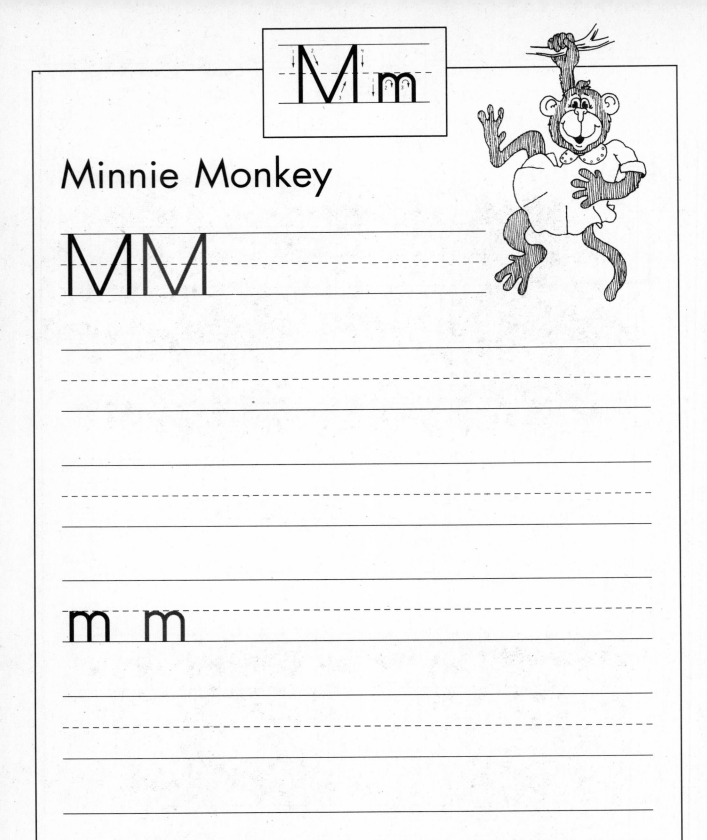

Minnie Monkey

M M

m m

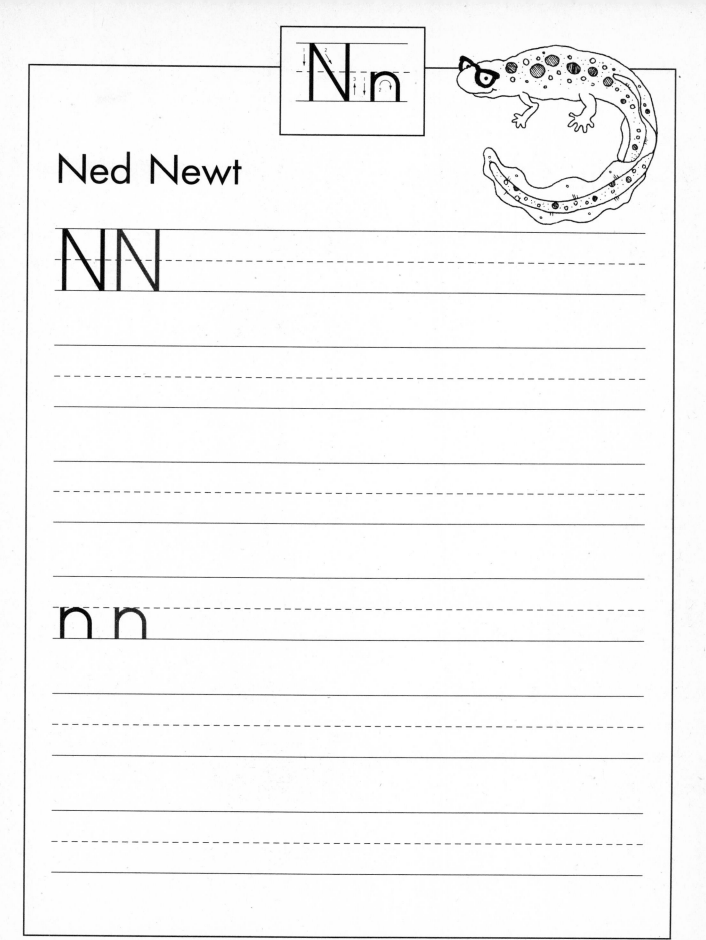

Ned Newt

N N

n n

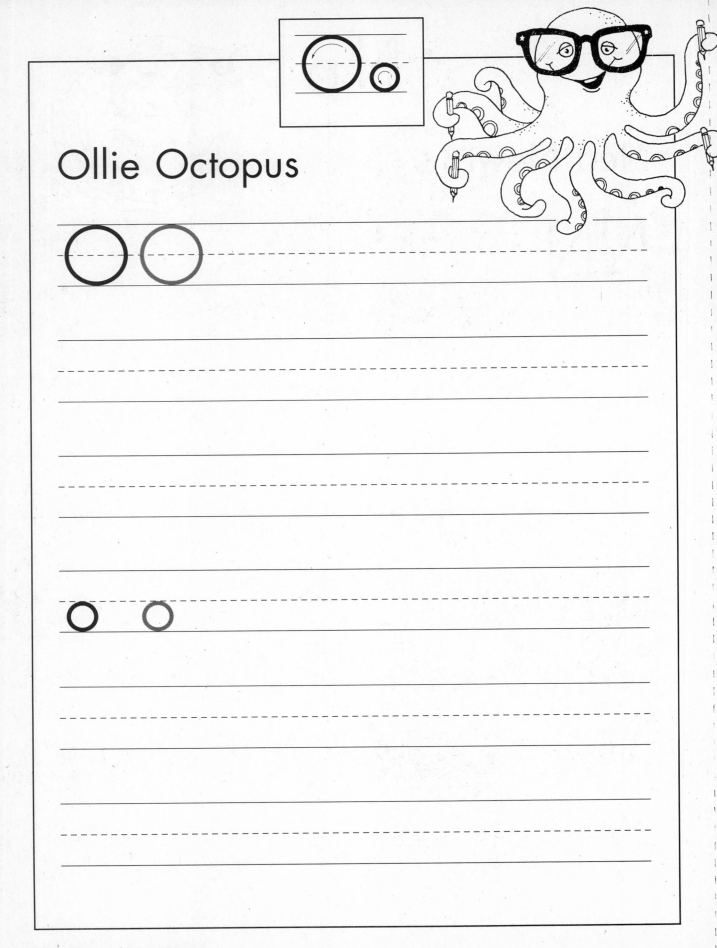

Ollie Octopus

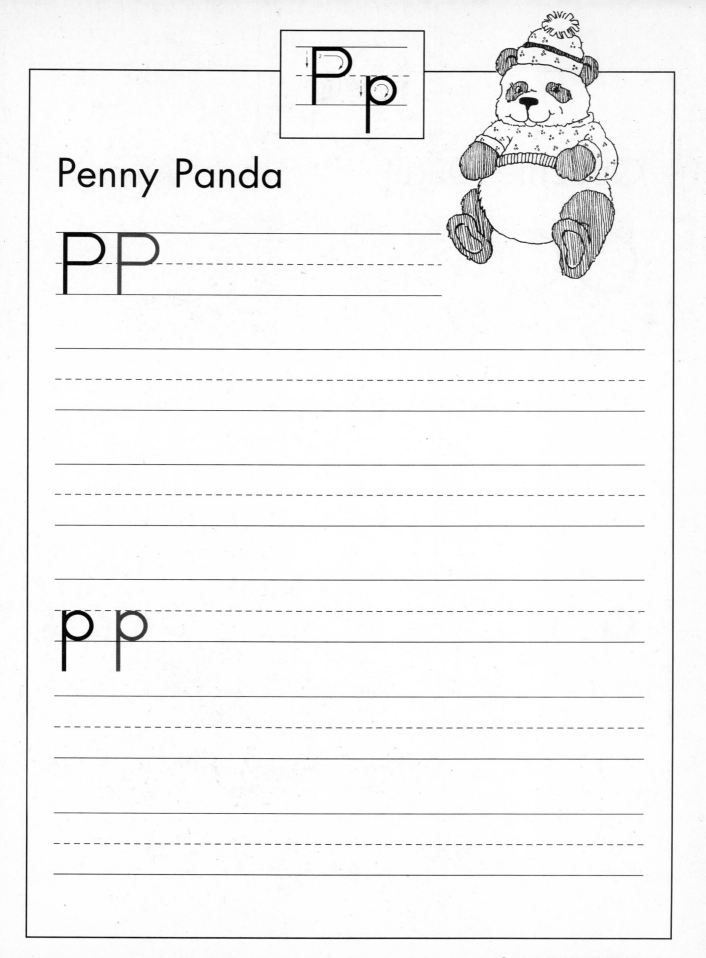

Penny Panda

P P

p p

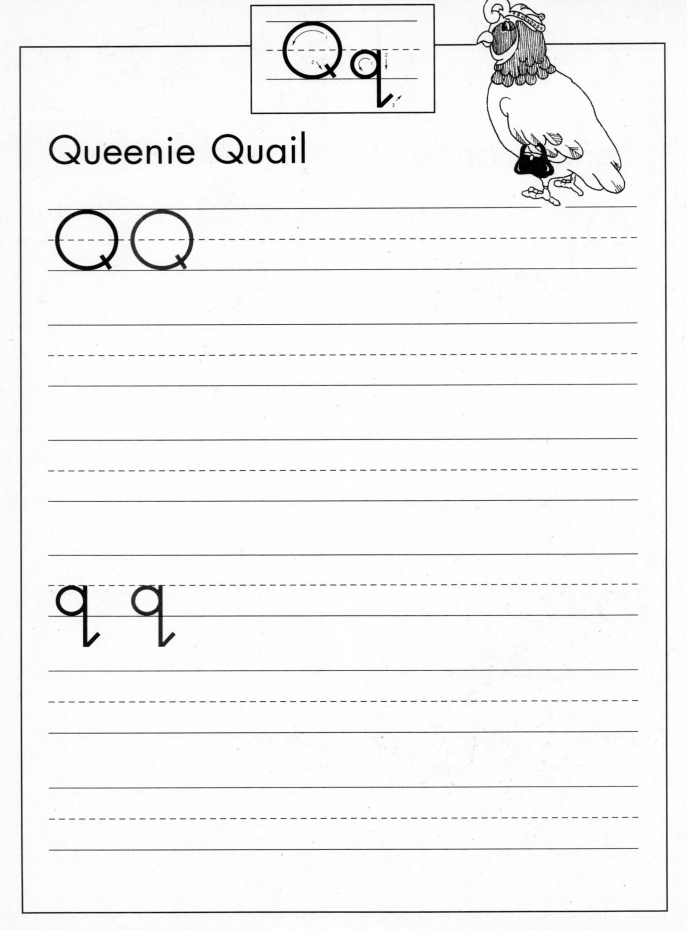

Queenie Quail

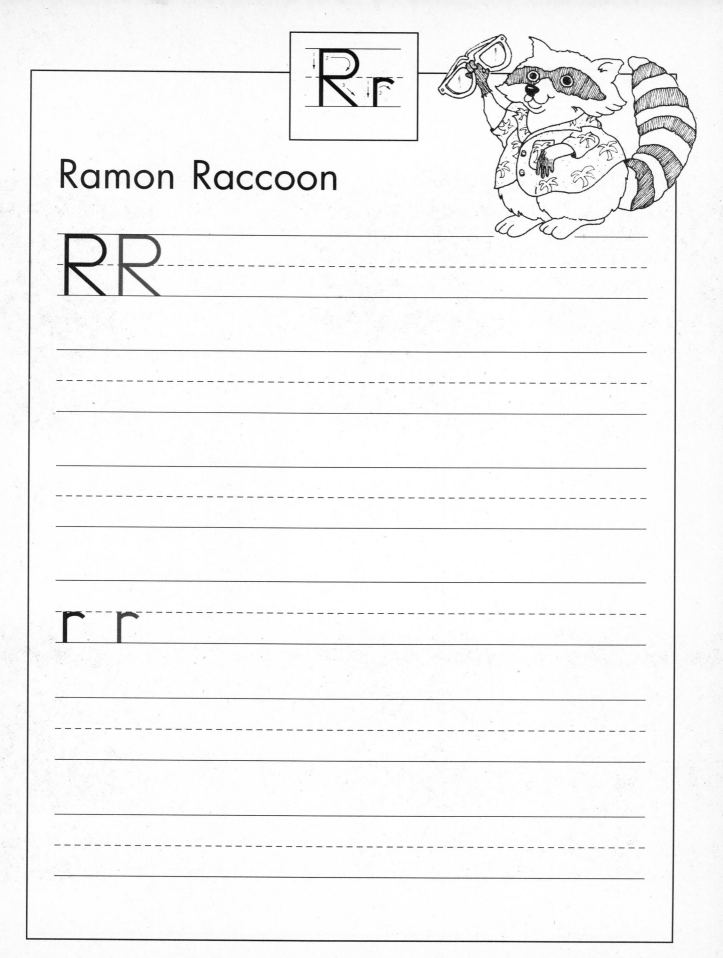

Ramon Raccoon

R R

r r

Slippy Seal

S S

s s

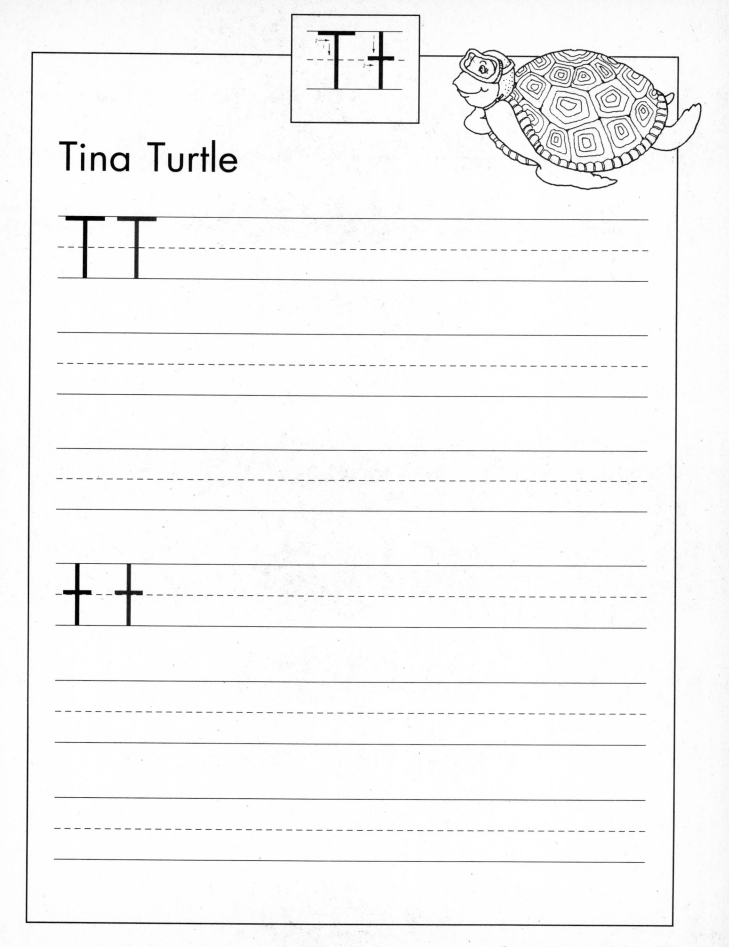

Tina Turtle

T T

t t

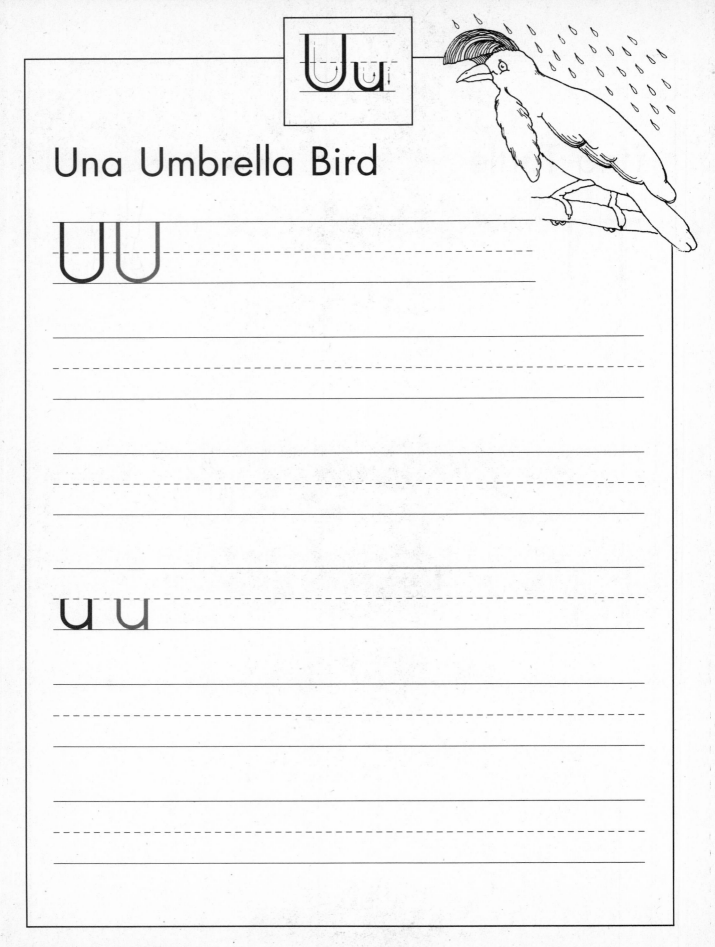

Una Umbrella Bird

U U

u u

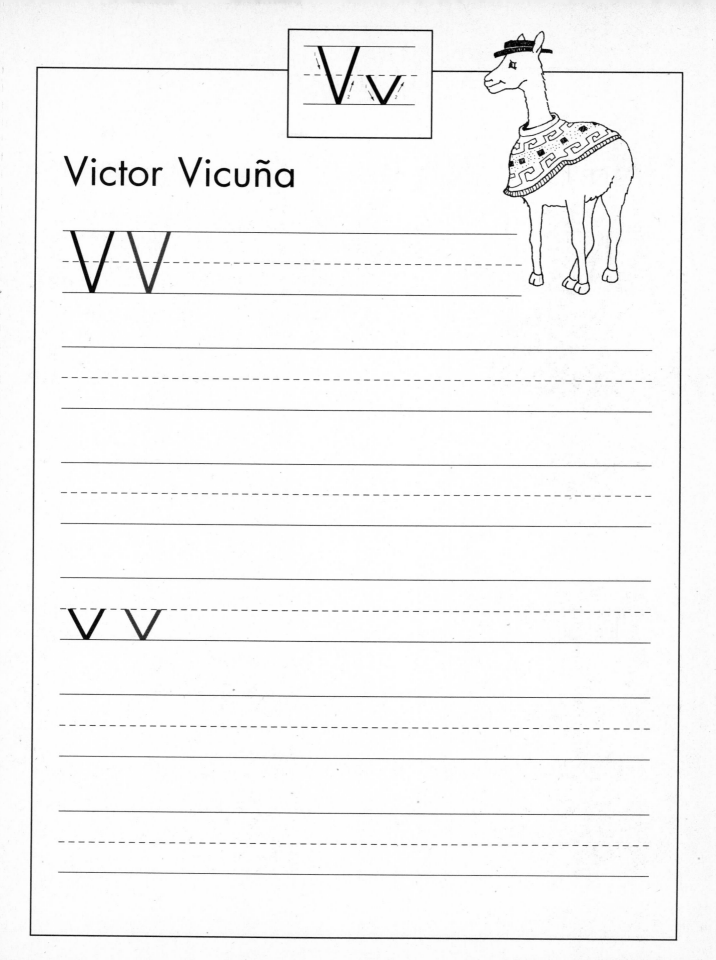

Victor Vicuña

V V

v v

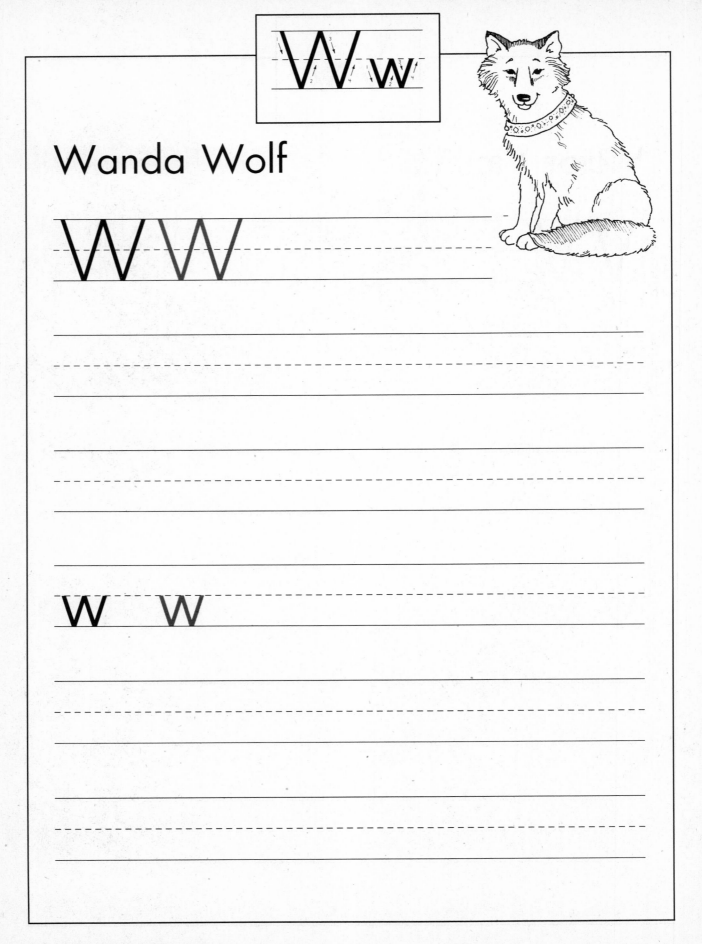

Wanda Wolf

W W

w w

Felipe Fox

X x

X X

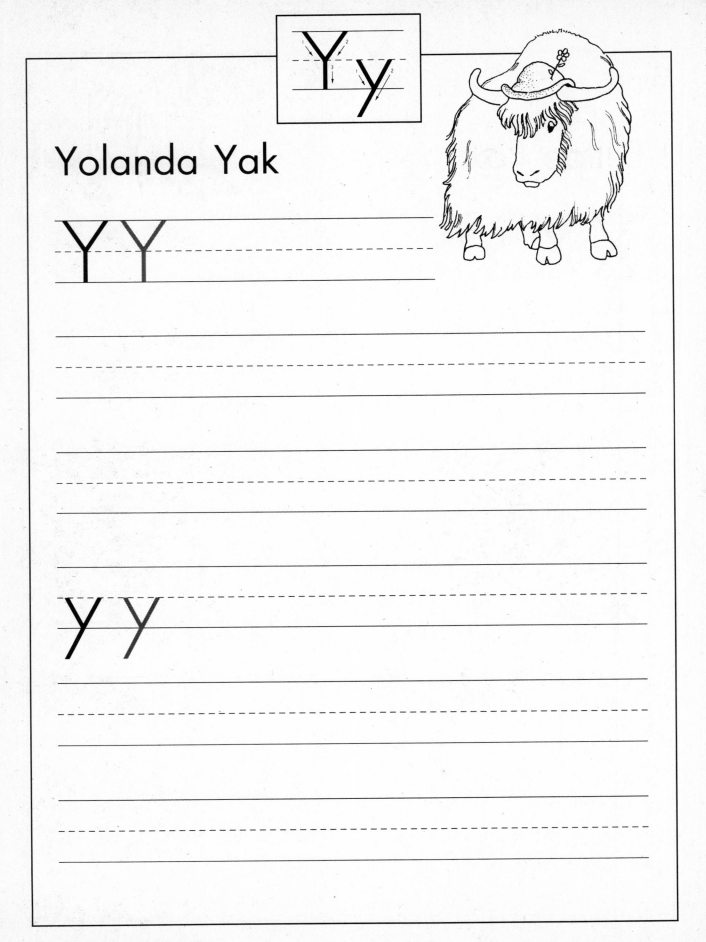

Yolanda Yak

Y Y

y y

Zippy Zebra

Z Z

Z Z

HANDWRITING CERTIFICATE

I Am a Handwriting Star

Name

Grade

Age